WITHDRAWN

The Common Curriculum

Routledge Education Books

Advisory editor: John Eggleston
Professor of Education
University of Keele

The Common Curriculum
Its Structure and Style in the Comprehensive School

Maurice Holt

Routledge & Kegan Paul
London, Henley and Boston

First published in 1978
by Routledge & Kegan Paul Ltd
39 Store Steet,
London WC1E 7DD,
Broadway House,
Newtown Road,
Henley-on-Thames,
Oxon RG9 1EN and
9 Park Street,
Boston, Mass. 02108, USA
Set by Hope Services, Wantage
and printed in Great Britain by
Lowe & Brydone Ltd

British Library Cataloguing in Publication Data

Holt, Maurice

The Common Curriculum. – (Routledge education books).
1. Education, Secondary – England – Curricula
I. Title
373.1'9'0942 LB1629.5.G7 78–40090

ISBN 0-7100-8895-7

Contents

Foreword

One of the sad features of the current debate on education is the gap between theory and practice. Many teachers and head teachers regard themselves as 'good practical types' who get on with the job and leave theory to others. Maurice Holt was an exception in this respect: when he became Headmaster of Sheredes School in the late 1960s he was already familiar with a good deal of theoretical work about comprehensive schools and curriculum planning; since then he has had ample opportunity to put theory into practice and add to the theory by his own writings.

I first got to know the school and Maurice Holt in 1973 when I became the University representative on the Governing Body. I was immediately impressed by the curriculum and organisation of the school. There was a sense of order and purpose among the pupils which is so often lacking in secondary schools. Not only is the curriculum well planned but, by and large, the pupils see the point of it as well and react to it as something which is worthwhile and relevant. This book is much more than a description of one successful school, however. It is a highly critical discussion of curriculum research and the English secondary school system. Out of this emerges Maurice Holt's practical recommendation for a common curriculum. This is a common curriculum with choice within the core subjects rather than between subjects with equal claims. Premature specialisation is avoided and the choices that the pupils make are well informed and likely to be met.

Foreword

I hope this book will be read by parents and others interested in education as well as educationists. It is refreshingly free from jargon and discusses a number of difficult issues in a way which any intelligent adult could enjoy.

Denis Lawton

Professor of Curriculum Studies
University of London Institute of Education

Preface

I began writing this book in my last term as head of Sheredes School, and finished it in my first as a curriculum consultant. What began, and ended, as an attempt to take a fresh look at the curriculum and organisation of the comprehensive school has inevitably been influenced by the contributions to the 'great debate' on education that has been launched and sustained during that time. While I hope, therefore, that the book shows some awareness of current issues, at the same time I have noticed that my central concern from the beginning with the potentialities of the common curriculum has been reinforced by sympathetic echoes from a variety of sources. And it seems clearer than ever to me that if we take a common curriculum to mean a school-based programme of development which will initiate all the school's pupils into key aspects of our culture, then we must see it as an effective way in which the hitherto untapped possibilities of the comprehensive school can be realised.

I hope, though, to have avoided the temptation to which book-writing heads are prone: to offer one uniquely right way of designing a curriculum and running a school. Since the curriculum and development of Sheredes School is unusual and on the whole a successful development from existing practice, I am bound to refer to it, and the more readily since I know it well; but I apologise in advance if an over-sanguine tone should creep in. I have tried to consider the particular only in the context of the general, and I ask to be forgiven for using case-study material that is most easily to hand.

Perhaps I should add that I am one who moved from technological research in industry to teaching mathematics in an independent boarding school, and caught the ferment for comprehensive education in the early 1960s. Coming from the independent sector to an established, first-generation comprehensive school at that time seems, in retrospect, to reflect the idealism of the period; at the same time, my absence of experience in any kind of selective maintained school meant that I came fresh and optimistic to the comprehensive. And after eight years of establishing a new kind of comprehensive, my optimism for the future of the common school is as strong as ever.

Clyst William House
Plymtree
Cullompton, Devon.

June 1977

Acknowledgments

I should like to thank all the staff of Sheredes School, Hertfordshire who, during the seven years from its opening with first-year pupils in 1969 to its fulfilment with a compplete sixth-form in 1976, made it possible by their industry and inventiveness to establish a common curriculum in a comprehensive school; and the parents and governors who gave such wholehearted support to new ideas and demanding activities. The following colleagues were particularly helpful in providing curriculum detail, directly or indirectly: Brenda Llewellin (sixth form), David Martin, Sue Mathews, Terry Lowry, Jane Clements, Lesley Buckley and Nigel Robbins (humanities), Libby Mountford and Peter Bosley (English), Caryl Ventham, John Mitchell, David Deacon and Lindsay Robertshaw (expressive arts), Tony Dickens and Keith Nancekievill (mathematics), Chris Connop and Bill Spicer (modern languages), Jim Chapman, Chris Kitchin and Phil Winstanley (science), Allan Sutton and Shirley Storey (physical activities), Joy Gray (careers and counselling), Michael Swain, John Akers and Charles Harper (creative activities) and Mary Stableford (remedial studies). Of these, I am greatly indebted to David Martin who, as my deputy, contributed so much to our discussions and to the implementation of curriculum change. And without the administrative skills of my secretary, Daphne Jones, there would have been little time for discussion or implementation.

Finally, I am particularly grateful to Joy Gray for reading and commenting on the manuscript, and to Professor Denis

Lawton for his encouragement as a governor of Sheredes School, his valuable advice on the final draft and his kindness in offering to write a foreword to this book.

Chapter 1

Where We Are Now:

Realities and Constraints

This is a book about secondary education and, in particular, about the way it can be extended to all pupils in comprehensive schools. It is not too soon to recognise that the development of comprehensive education upwards from 11 is the major educational advance of the second half of this century; we can also look back on the first stage in the evolution of the comprehensive school and see what can be learnt from a decade of intensive growth. It is a good moment to consider what patterns of organisation have emerged, and examine the underlying educational ideas which have given rise to these patterns. We must look at the answers the schools have derived to two key questions: What should the pupils learn? And how can this learning best be brought about? We shall, therefore, need to look at both theory and practice; and in the light of their present state, we can go on to discuss the shape of the curriculum and organisation of the next generation of comprehensive schools.

We have certainly lived through a period of great educational activity, fired by the ideal of universal education. Ruskin (in *Time and Tide*) recognised that this would not be easily achieved:

> I hold it for indisputable, that the first duty of a State is to see that every child born therein shall be well housed, clothed, fed, and educated, till it attain years of discretion. But in order to effect this the Government must have an authority over the people of which we now do not so much as dream.

The political force of the ideal is such that, given the economic means, the dream was bound to be realised in the end; and the most likely explanation of the present feeling that the dream has gone a little sour is simply the harsher financial climate. The prospect of further cuts in educational budgets might seem the worst possible time to propose changes. But it is a time when value for money really matters, and when there is a mood of accountability in the air. A feeling of questioning and a need for retrenchment might, paradoxically, give the right ambience for promoting a new certainty of purpose and effect. Let us, therefore, see where we are at present, and how we have got there.

The Present State

Perhaps 1964 was the year when the comprehensive reform seemed most persuasive. By the early 1960s both the then Conservative Education Minister (Boyle) and the future Labour Minister (Crosland) were speaking in similar language about the need to widen opportunity, and the right of all children to acquire intelligence. 1964 saw, too, the foundation of the Schools Council at Boyle's instigation, and it is arguable that Crosland's Circular 10/65 had little direct effect on the growth of comprehensive schools; the momentum was already there. Indeed, John Vaizey has suggested that a tougher instrument than Circular 10/65 might have seen the completion of the entire reform in short order, such was the favourable groundswell of middle-class opinion.

In the ten years from 1964 the number of comprehensive schools increased tenfold, from 250 to 2,500 approximately (Benn and Simon, 1972). The same ten years saw the first cycle of curriculum development in this country, starting with the announcement of the Nuffield Science Teaching Project in 1962, and ending with the marketing of teaching materials derived from a plethora of Schools Council Projects. It was a decade when education became an industry, with curriculum studies one of the most buoyant sectors. On the one hand, secondary reorganisation schemes were promoting a major change in the structure of schooling; on the other, the curriculum development programme was a major field of research growth, aimed at 'the systematic planning, production and use of new practice' (MacDonald and Walker, 1976). And in between, one might expect to see the new comprehensives seizing the opportunity to develop new approaches to the curriculum.

The reality has been rather different. As Lawton (1973) remarks, one reason is that

> the Spens formula of three kinds of children/three kinds of schools . . . has perpetuated an elitist mentality. The second disappointment has been the consistent failure to re-think the curriculum and plan a programme which would be appropriate for universal secondary education.

It is easy to conclude that, on the whole, not much has changed. The parent whose child is in the first year of the local comprehensive school (a true story, this) and has gone to the school bookshop to buy a dictionary, only to be asked by the sixth-former running it whether she is in the top stream or the bottom stream, since each stream has a different one, may well have decided that comprehensive education is not synonymous with comprehensive schooling. And if he were to look at the overflowing shelves of an educational bookshop and note the torrent of descriptions and prescriptions that the curriculum industry has spawned, he might marvel that so much theory has produced so little change in practice.

An important factor is that support for comprehensive education arose from the way the 1944 Education Act worked out, rather than from any cogent advocacy in the Act itself. It is certainly reasonable, as Lawton (1975) suggests, to see the Act 'as evidence of a dramatic change of attitude . . . the principle of equality of opportunity was established even if the realisation was still extremely difficult'; but attempts to realise the principle were almost entirely conceived in terms of two distinctive traditions of schooling. While the Norwood Report 1943 had conveniently reinforced the Spens Report 1938 doctrine of three kinds of pupils – academic, technical and 'practical' – for three kinds of schools, the intermediate technical schools appeared in only a few urban areas and those responsible for administering the 1944 Act were content to see a new flowering of the grammar school on the one hand, and of the secondary modern as a refurbished version of the old senior elementary school on the other.

The grammar school, with fee-paying abolished, now became a much more selective institution than before; for the idea of different kinds of pupils had subtly shifted to that of different ranges of ability. And although a White Paper issued by the Board of Education in 1943, *Educational Reconstruction*, had stated: 'There is nothing to be said in favour of a system which subjects children at the age of eleven to the strain of a competitive examination on which, not only their future schooling, but their future careers may depend', just such a system was being used to select the 20 per cent going to grammar schools, and the 5 per cent to the ill-starred technical schools. The remaining 75 per cent started their secondary school careers as failures, in spite of the hollow doctrine of 'parity of esteem' for the secondary moderns.

This story has been told in detail by Rubinstein and Simon (1969) and only the outline is appropriate here. The point is that the reconstructionist theme of the early 1940s – secondary education for all – had become, by the end of that decade, different kinds of secondary education for all. Dissatisfaction with that state of affairs became the political mainspring leading to the comprehensive school. The contributory reasons are worth summarising. At root, of course, was mistrust of the intelligence tests used for the 11-plus transfer. Eventually, in 1957, a working party of the British Psychological Society rejected the Hadow-Spens theories of differentiation, and recommended that selection at the age of ten or eleven could no longer be justified on psychological grounds; intelligence was partly a result of environmental stimulation. But it would be a mistake to regard psychologists as the villains of the piece; theirs is a field of inquiry which can scarcely be regarded as an exact science, and their theories will, in the nature of things, wax and wane with the ebb and flow of research and dialectic. The fatal error was to put such unswerving trust in one particular theory; and the error was exposed because it was used, in effect, as the basis for legislation.

Burt's work on intelligence testing was of great importance in making the mills of selection grind efficiently, yet he deserves credit for rebutting the way the Norwood report shifted the ground from his theories of innate difference in intelligence, to distinctions between alleged different types of child. This was the pivot about which the doctrine of tripartism turned; and in its Norwood exegesis, the conclusion was that different types of child need different types of curriculum. It should be noted, though, that in the event it didn't quite come out like that; the post-1944 argument and implementation centred on types of organisation. The key questions about what ought to be in the curriculum, for whatever type of school, were never on the surface of the debate.

The influence of type of school had been brought out by Vernon (1957), who showed that the IQs of pupils in Southampton who were selected for grammar and technical schools rose by 4.9 points over three or four years, while those of pupils in modern schools fell by three points. This could be attributed to the poorer intellectual stimulus of the modern schools; and another factor was the established association of the grammar schools with middle-class parents, and of the modern schools with the working class.

In spite of this, some modern schools had entered voluntary fifth-year pupils for O-level examinations with considerable success, and this brought home to aspiring parents the arbitrariness of a decision at eleven which excluded a considerable number of children, despite inter-school transfers, from the sought-after privilege of a grammar-school education. As a corollary of this, the grammar-school curriculum was accepted as good virtually by definition; why bother to change it, when everyone wants to get into it? Even though national figures for the proportion of grammar school pupils continuing with post-16 education, and for the performance of working-class pupils, showed these schools guilty of a remarkable degree of inadequacy and waste, their vociferous supporters (like Eric, now Lord, James, see Benn and Simon, 1972) were able to make exactly opposite claims and, on the whole, get away with it. The position is much the same today, even though the shortcomings of the grammar-school curriculum have been remarked on by such writers as Hirst (1967). This poses not only an external threat to the comprehensive school but also, as we shall see, an internal influence on its organisation.

And against the presumption of classical correctness for the work of the grammar school were set vague platitudes for that of the secondary modern. 'Free from the pressure of any external examination, these schools can work out the best and liveliest forms of secondary education *suited to their pupils*. It is essential that they should retain *this invaluable freedom* . . . and should be enabled to advance along the lines *they themselves feel to be right*' (*The Nation's Schools*, Ministry of Education, 1945: my italics). The polarities are plain. On the one hand the grammar school, secure in its university affiliations and attenuated public-school traditions, is plugged into a permanent set of external values; on the other is an open-handed invitation to base a curriculum on internal values, on teachers' perceptions of children's needs. It is my thesis that exactly these two paradigms have been carried over into most present-day comprehensive schools; and that neither is right.

All this gave rise to the kind of widely expressed feelings which led ultimately to political decisions; or, as Tawney put it in another context, educational policy is always social policy. By the late 1950s some device was needed to give more substance to the notion of equal opportunity latent in the 1944 Act, and minimise the painful side-effects of selection by testing. Some early comprehensive schools already existed, and Pedley's 1955 survey of them gave a favourable picture. We shall consider why they were there in the next chapter. Their effect must have been encouraging, but it would be wrong to suppose that positive support for their educational character led to a mass demand for more of them. It was rather that negative support for the social and educational ill-effects of the tripartite system led to a search for alternatives; for what has been termed a comprehensive local system, perhaps, rather than a comprehensive school. The lack, in the popular consciousness, of a distinct desire for comprehensive schools for their own sake (along the lines of, for example, that for home ownership) explains both the piecemeal pattern of subsequent development and the ease with which, in recent times, support for them can be undermined in some particular local set-piece. Although a sociologist might look back and remark, 'The broad base of the original comprehensive campaign, once a source of powerful political support, is now splintering' (Marsden, 1970), it is problematic how broad a base this ever was. This is why, twelve years after the publication of an enterprising book like Armstrong and Young's *The Flexible School*, it feels just as if it came out yesterday. The arguments have flowed changelessly back and forth over the same old ground like trench warfare on the Somme, to as little purpose and for much the same reason; neither side has as yet a massive juggernaut which can sweep all aside and break the deadlock. Happily, though, the general drift is in the right direction.

One of the first extensive comprehensive local systems was that of Leicestershire (1957), and the Plan and its developments have proved successful. With the comprehensive school defined in 1947 (circular 144) only in the loosest terms (a school 'which is intended to cater for all the secondary education of all the children in a given area, without organisation into three sides'), and without any luminous exemplar of what such a school should be, local education authorities have gone on to produce a variety of schemes depending on the particular local mix of politics, buildings and enthusiasm (or lack of it). But the predominant type has been the 11–18 all-through school, and still is, and it is with this type of school that this book is mainly concerned.

Theory

We have looked at the origins of the general movement in the late 1950s towards comprehensive local systems, leading to ten years of considerable growth from 1964 which coincided with a great expansion in curriculum studies, partly as a theoretical activity but with curriculum development as its practical arm. An attempt will be made to gauge the influence of this activity on the way comprehensive schools look at their curricula.

One way to start is to look at curriculum studies now, at a time when there is a general feeling of taking stock: due not least to the money running out. Writing in 1975 of curriculum changes in the field of educational studies, Stenhouse says: 'This change . . . has increased the rigour and the intellectual tone of education courses. It has done little for their relevance to the problem of improving the practice of teaching.' And, later: 'the crucial problem for curriculum research and study is the development of theory and methodology which is subservient to the needs of teachers and schools. This means that the theory has to be accessible.' The message seems clear and unexceptionable. The trouble is that the subservience and access are not often in evidence in the field of curriculum studies.

It is disappointing, if true, to read that 'philosophy by itself can yield no practical prescriptions: nor, in the current state of our understanding, can educational theory' (Sockett, 1976). Those who have to make things work in schools are less interested, after ten years of them, in hearing about the issues and the questions; it is naive to expect precise answers, but it is important that theoretical studies should be less effete and remote, and more closely geared, in structure and substance, to education as a practical process. For we certainly need theories of curriculum development; we need to make critical and reflective use of them in the context of the school. It would be a disaster if theoretical studies became the real secret garden of the curriculum; an ornamental orangery raising inedible fruits, rather than a part of everyday school consciousness.

This sort of thing happens when the research field lacks tested principles and rules of inquiry. The sickness has been diagnosed by Schwab (1969): 'The field of curriculum is moribund, unable by its present methods and principles to continue its work and desperately in search of new and more effective principles and methods.' Schwab distinguishes between the discipline of the practical, concerned with choice and action, and that of the theoretic, concerned with knowledge. He argues cogently that 'a large bulk of curriculum energies must be diverted from the theoretic, not only to the eclectic but to the practical' and favours a commitment to a process of deliberation leading to defensible decisions rather than the warranted conclusions of the theoretic.

It is debatable whether many research studies are irrelevant, as Schwab would argue, or just plain specious, as has been suggested by Kitwood (1976): he has discovered that much educational research makes erroneous, sub-scientific assumptions about aims and methods and concludes that 'a large body of educational research is misconceived . . . and that those who are sceptical or ignore it, preferring to use commonsense, trial and error, and the accumulated insights of the practitioners of their craft, are following a wise intuition.' Noting that researchers tend to blame the failure of teachers to attend to research findings on their conservatism, he suggests an alternative explanation: that teachers are concerned 'with real events, not with measurements; with the actual attitude and morale of students, not with answers to arbitrarily framed questions; with the causes, not the correlates of academic success and failure.' A notorious, and dangerously misleading, example of research of this kind is Bennett's study (1976) *Teaching Styles and Pupil Progress*, which uses elaborate but questionnaire-based techniques in an attempt to compare quantitatively two quite different value systems; as if it were possible to demonstrate scientifically that it is more correct to be a Catholic than a Mormon.

None of this is meant to be a philistine attack on academic research; but it is certainly an attack on bad research. We are, after all, trying to see why research has so little influenced classroom practice, and one reason is the irrelevance or pitiful inadequacy of much of the stuff that is published. A recent surveyor of the field is Wilson (1975) who suggests for a start that much of the psychology, sociology and history that is currently drawn on to fuel the educational theory machine ought properly to be regarded as background studies; the central issue is 'human beings learning things or increasing their knowledge and rationality . . . education is connected to the development of understanding much as medicine is connected to health.' He draws a parallel between the present pre-theoretic state of curriculum and the pre-scientific period of alchemy: 'amidst a vast quantity of fantasy and superstition, intelligent men were working and interesting things being done – but, for lack of a clear idea and tradition of doing science, they would then have been difficult or impossible to identify.' The important point, though, is that Wilson's thesis is entirely a constructive one: urging the need for worthwhile theory, he adds: 'the disaster lies in the severance of the practical skills from any serious or sustained consideration of a more general or theoretical kind.'

This position is generally consonant with that of Schwab, but with a clearer statement than Schwab's of the underpinning role that the right sort of educational theory would have. Both Wilson and Schwab regard present attempts at a theory of curriculum as either simplistic or wrong-headed. Perhaps the two best-known of these are termed by Stenhouse (1975) the objectives model – derived from the Tyler/Taba pioneering means-end approach, with the aid of Bloom's behavioural taxonomy – and the process model, based rather on principles of procedure and avoiding pre-specified outcomes. Aspects of both will be considered in Chapter 3. If our analysis so far is right, the greater affinity of the process model to deliberative intervention in the school itself is likely to make it the more useful. A similar point has been made by Reid in Reid and Walker (1975), concluding a survey of a number of British and American case studies of curriculum change:

> To try to deny this complexity and to see curriculum change as something which can be conceptualised in simple, mechanistic terms, is not merely to invoke an alien theory, it is also to import a rigid and antipathetic dogmatism into an activity which, our case studies suggest, depends for its effectiveness on consensus, negotiation and deliberation.

My hope is to show how such an activity can be established, making use of that educational theory which seems to be necessary, worthwhile and available.

So much, though, for dissatisfaction with attempts at a general theory of curriculum. What of the effect of the range of curriculum development projects mounted since the early 1960s? In some ways the first of them all – the Nuffield Science Teaching Project – has been most widely adopted and had the deepest impact. But it is unusual to find a school that has not modified the Nuffield materials – or even its philosophy – in some way. The original impetus here came from the teachers themselves – the Science Masters' Association – and could be seen as continuing an innovating tradition. The separate O-level subject projects in physics, chemistry and biology were published in 1967, to be followed by Combined Science in 1970. The latter has gained wide acceptance in the first two years of comprehensive schooling; the influence of the former is greater, in that it has reinforced the notion of science in separate subject compartments as soon as the real thing – O-level exams – looms near. To some extent it has become a new orthodoxy, and advocates of an integrated approach have to work hard to get science teachers to take a broader perspective. This illustrates the need to bear project developments in mind when considering the general state of curriculum theory in schools; the influence tends to come through.

Perhaps the most influential project was a private venture rather than an institutional product. With money raised from industry, and with the entrepreneurial flair of its director, Bryan Thwaites, the School Mathematics Project moved from its cradle in a group of independent schools to infiltrate a large proportion of grammar and comprehensive schools. The original numbered texts, appearing in the early 1960s, were a remarkable innovation in a conservative profession. Although awkwardness of language and sequence have led to their relegation in favour of the later lettered books, they were the result of practical teaching experience of largely unfamiliar topics. It is not difficult to think of Schools Council Projects that laboured longer, and more expensively, and produced a mouse in comparison. A more detailed consideration of SMP, and of Nuffield Science, will be given in Chapter 7. It is only worth noting here that an analysis of the SMP main school course by Malpas (1974) suggests that there is an imbalance between the language function of mathematics, as an abstract tool, and its modelling function when applied to specific situations. An important cause of the difficulties experienced in schools stems from failures in the underlying curriculum model, showing again the need for a sound theoretical basis for curriculum development projects.

The Schools Council projects have been extensively published, but their impact in schools has been surprisingly slight. Some, like Keele Integrated Studies or Project Technology, have suffered from a certain fatal diffidence of approach and are rarely met with; and one wonders what there is to show for the £892,000 (not all from Council funds) lavished on the Modern Languages Project. Despite much publicity, the controversial Humanities Curriculum Project seems to have a greater fascination for curriculum buffs than for teachers in schools. And many of the Reports have suffered from a desire to face all ways at once and offend none; the tortured prose and fractured logic of the Working Paper on the Whole Curriculum is a sad example. Sad but not surprising because, as White (1969) pointed out some time ago, the Council has inclined to a piecemeal, subject-centred view of the curriculum, and most projects have been conceived in terms of only part of the ability range. It is often forgotten that the Humanities Project was one such.

There have been, too, some most useful projects and Reports: of the latter, those on Religious Education in Secondary Schools, and on Social Studies 8–13, stand out for clear thinking imbued with practical common sense. The Cambridge School Classics Project developed non-linguistic materials of considerable value in the early years of humanities courses, and the Integrated Science Project showed prescience and classroom effectiveness. We now have the view of the DES that the Schools Council's curriculum performance has been mediocre, and certainly its engagement between projects and schools has never been strong. The tradition of school autonomy, unsympathetic LEAs, and the weakness of the Research, Development and Diffusion Model used chiefly as the basis of project strategy are all factors. And its overwhelming teacher representation has reflected uncertainties in the schools themselves. But the real deficiency has been the lack of any systematic policy of curriculum development, supported by theoretical considerations and based on an appreciation of the educational values underlying secondary schooling. Perhaps this positive leadership would have been more in evidence if senior personnel were able to stay longer in their posts. It would have helped, too, if the DES had made some attempt to develop a clear understanding of the educational purpose of the comprehensive school.

Practice

This brings us to consider the present state of comprehensive education in action. The general pattern is easily stated. In the absence of any educational directive, comprehensives have simply tried to assimilate the two existing traditions derived from the grammar and modern schools. They make uneasy bedfellows since one, as has been pointed out, suffers from a rigid view of objectives in terms of O-level and A-level courses, and the other from a vagueness about objectives and loose-thinking about children's wants and needs.

There may, in the first year or two of schooling, be a common curriculum; but genuine non-streaming is not often found. More frequently pupils are grouped in two, sometimes three bands by ability, with mixed-ability groups within the bands. Many schools band in this way, yet perversely deny the charge of streaming. It is hard to penetrate logic of this kind. Setting within the bands is common for mathematics and French, and sometimes even for English. And by the third year, the need to introduce a second foreign language is often the excuse for making the divided curriculum manifest for all to see.

The inevitable pattern in years 4 and 5 is to run a small common core alongside an extensive series of option subjects, usually grouped in from five to seven columns. The core will include English, physical education and religious education (strictly, of course, a statutory requirement) and perhaps a tutorial or careers period to make about 20 per cent of the timetable in all. Entry to option subjects is usually conditional on staff recommendations, and always on the number of staff and places available, so that in practice it is no surprise to discover that the old bipartite structure is alive and well and living in the option columns. Somehow it turns out that abler pupils will take their usual diet of 8 or 9 O-level subjects, while the less-able find themselves spending part of the time at nearby colleges of further education pursuing courses aimed at introducing them to the world of work. Nothing could show more clearly how the two traditions, of one school for the managers and another for the hewers of wood and drawers of water, live on unchanging.

An NFER survey, *A Matter of Choice* (Reid, 1974), examined option schemes of this kind more closely in a sample of schools. The survey looked at the reasons pupils gave for choosing option subjects, and how the pupils viewed their choices in the fourth year when they had had time to assess them:

> Around 40% of the fourth formers were either dissatisfied with or indifferent towards their elected subjects; there were marked differences in satisfaction between pupils of different abilities. Using teacher assessments, it was estimated that some 40% were in fact being taught in groups which did not correspond to their capabilities for two or more subjects . . . Again, misplacement was far more common among the less bright children. When the structure of

the school was examined it was found that allocation to a particular stream or band, or choices made even before the third year, considerably limited the opportunities open to some pupils. Dissatisfaction with choice was found to relate to other behaviours and attitudes; ill-suited children tended to have poorer attendance records, intended to leave earlier and saw school as a rigid, purposeless and constraining community.

Yet it is of just this kind of system that Schools Council Working Paper 53 remarked: '(pupils in the fourth and fifth years) should be allowed choice on the grounds that one of the aims of secondary education is to prepare and encourage pupils to take increasing responsibility for themselves. How better to realize this aim than to allow pupils a degree of discretion over what they spend their time on in school?' The fallacy here is the assumption that choice must be exercised between subjects, rather than within curriculum-areas. The reality of such systems is exposed all too clearly in the NFER research quoted. But there are other objections. Such schemes tend to be expensive to staff, because of the proliferation of small teaching groups, and this is usually achieved at the expense of larger groups in the first three years. Yet it is in those years that most richness is needed; where overlooking the difficulties of individual pupils will lead to behavioural problems in years 4 and 5. Another disadvantage is that pastoral work in the third year inevitably revolves around the impending option scheme, and takes the form of trying to make premature assumptions about the pupil's interests and career choices rather than a discussion of what he is like, there and then.

Most seriously, though, these option schemes prevent any genuine concept of a balanced education from prevailing. There is evidence that far too many pupils are suffering from premature specialisation, so that their choices on entering the sixth form are effectively determined by those they made in the third form. Some option-based comprehensives attempt to mitigate this by insisting that at least one science subject is taken, or at least one art and craft subject. This misses the point. Curriculum balance cannot be seen just in terms of subjects; if the aim is to give pupils an understanding of the nature of the scientific process, it is not going to be met by requiring a pupil to take CSE human biology, however admirable a course that may be in itself. If the aim is to give some understanding of physical and human science a course with a much broader, yet just as penetrating, base is needed. For abler pupils, option schemes are notorious for generating difficulties in the matter of choices in the areas of science and languages. Most grammar-school curricula suffer from this problem, and the divisive structure of first-generation comprehensives repeats the errors. As a rule, only those who are virtually science specialists at the age of 13 will find themselves doing all three sciences to O-level; if they happen to be good enough to tackle a couple of foreign languages they will be the victims of an inter-departmental tug-of-war. And any continuing contact with the world of aesthetics is out of the question; crafts are for the non-academic, while art, though respectable, is strictly for artists. For less-able pupils, the option choices present a different problem. What exactly goes on in film studies, or good grooming, or design for living, or communication? Titles like this usually describe well-meaning, but seriously undemanding, courses inspired more by a desire to keep pupils quiet while filling up the time than to initiate them into some worthwhile form of knowledge.

Alongside this kind of academic organisation, it is customary to find a heavy emphasis on pastoral care. This term refers to the arrangements made to look after the personal welfare of pupils, and is extended to the wider sense of bringing them to, or maintaining them in, a suitably tractable state so that they may profit from the school's programme of academic activities. Some go further and see it as including home visits and intimate links between school and community. Without doubt, this sort of provision makes a sharp contrast with the casual way in which the grammar school provided the lessons, but took no interest in what happened between or outside them apart from cricket and rugby matches and the annual Gilbert and Sullivan, or Shakespeare play.

In many comprehensives, then, there are several posts of considerable seniority for heads of houses or years, of lower, middle or upper school and so on. A school counsellor may also be appointed, possibly free of teaching commitments. These arrangements will be discussed in more detail in Chapter 9.

All we need note here is that provision of this kind may be quite extensive, and absorb a substantial proportion of promotion points and teaching time allocation. Further, there is a widespread view that pastoral care is the kind of good thing of which we cannot have too much. As I write, I notice a letter in an educational journal from a headmaster to complain of allegedly inaccurate reporting of a bullying incident at his comprehensive school. He ends with the remark 'a comprehensive school is as strong as its pastoral system'. Statements of this kind can usually be expected to pass unchallenged. But if only because resources in a school are limited, and likely to become more so, it is necessary to look at the extent of each kind of provision and consider its effectiveness.

But there is a further point that has more serious implications. The NFER research on choice in years 4 and 5 showed that 'Dissatisfaction with choice was found to relate to other behaviours and attitudes.' In other words, curriculum devices can generate patterns of disaffected behaviour which the pastoral-care system must then attempt to remedy. Or to put it still more bluntly, schools are demonstrably capable of manufacturing their own problems. There are, therefore, extremely good reasons for looking closely at the whole nature of the curriculum design, and the processes of teaching and learning, in a school; it may be that to say its strength lies in the pastoral system is to put faith in the stable door after the horse has bolted. For the moment, though, it is fair to say that the emphasis current practice places on pastoral care may be a distortion of important aspects of curriculum design, and may have deeper implications.

It is possible that the need for pastoral care first became evident because of the very large size of some of the earliest comprehensives. This occurred because it was originally thought that a school could be comprehensive only on an additive pattern; that is, by putting into it, side by side, a grammar, a technical and a modern mini-school. It was then reasoned that the size of the total school would be determined by the need to have a viable sixth form, which would come mainly from the grammar side, with perhaps a few from the technical. Hence the 2,000+ size of early comprehensives, which were really conceived as trilaterals, or bilaterals in some areas. The surprising thing is that this additive, as opposed to integrative, pattern of organisation has survived so remarkably in present comprehensives, of which the most common size will have about 800 to 900 pupils. Yet in the public consciousness, comprehensives are still thought of as large, and it is politically unwise to suggest that large schools are good. This probably reflects a general 'small is beautiful' trend rather than anything more specific. Indeed, research findings that suggest the larger school is worse than the smaller do not seem to exist. It is, however, true that the inherent advantages of the large school, in terms of choice of subjects and courses, are not in practice so easy to realise because of logistic problems arising from timetabling, staffing and accommodation.

We may have the large school to thank, too, for the interest shown over the last ten years in the application of commercial management techniques and concepts to the performance of senior roles in schools – particularly the head's. It can, of course, be argued with some force that management in industry and commerce is not merely an inexact science but a largely unsuccessful one; and the ethic of the market place is not the same as the set of moral principles governing the relationships between people with which the business of education is chiefly concerned. But there would seem to be scope in schools, none the less, for using analytical techniques, if only to improve the business and administrative side. These questions will be looked at in Chapter 5. At the moment, though, the fashionable book on school organisation will not be without its references to Burns and Stalker and other management theorists, and possibly flow-diagrams for good measure. But little of this is more than paper-deep. Perhaps the shrewdest comment on seeing the head's role in management terms comes from W. Taylor (1973):

> A school can be superbly 'managed', the process of consultation and decision making be smooth and trouble free, the relationships between local authority, governing body, head and staff harmonious, the fabric and accounts meticulously maintained, and morale among staff and pupils high. Yet, unless the concept of management is extended to include kinds of educational objectives that are extremely difficult to operationalise and evaluate, the work of that school can still represent failure.

Disillusionment with education in general, and the comprehensive schools in particular, has now reached the point where even the leader of a Labour government has called for a national debate, and the autonomy of individual schools and teachers may be subject to the intervention of HM Inspectorate. In particular, there is talk of establishing generally accepted principles for a core curriculum. This sounds like the right debate, but for the wrong reasons; for instrumental reasons, to do with schools meeting the needs of industry and society; rather than educational reasons, to do with civilisation and culture. It is good that at last questions about the curriculum of schools, rather than their structure and organisation, are to be faced. But the difficulties, as Taylor points out, are considerable if answers are to be sought merely in management approaches. The pressure is on to see accountability in quantitative terms, and the urge to measure is bureaucratically tempting if education is seen as useful to the state rather than life-enhancing for the individual. It is only too easy to devise tests and produce figures; it is quite another matter to identify desirable changes and see how to promote them.

It is perhaps significant that not much has been seen in the 1960s and 1970s of reforming chief education officers who, like Newsom or Morris, have conceived the task of schools in broader terms and recognised the importance of subtler kinds of educational objectives. There is now, more than at any time since the war, a need to look at education and the comprehensive school and try to see it whole. And parents, governors, teachers and administrators must all make the effort. Of the dissolution of the British Empire, A.J.P. Taylor has written: 'The British said that they were no longer strong enough to maintain their empire. It would be truer to say that they no longer believed in it. There is no explaining loss of belief of this kind. It happened.' We are far from losing our belief in comprehensive schools. But unless we can make them what they should be, rather than what they are, we shall lack the support we need to build them strong and keep them that way.

Chapter 2

Ideals and Possibilities: the Common Curriculum and a New Structure

The comprehensive school, it has been argued, took shape not from a clear educational vision, but from a political solution to the problem of pupil selection. So as the number of comprehensives grew, the chief reason for having them gained less force. And in the schools themselves, the main concern has been with problems of organisation rather than with basic purposes; with the how rather than with the why. Paradoxically, then, the more comprehensive schools took root, the less receptive has been the climate for an examination of first principles, and the more vulnerable are the schools to public criticism because, in the nature of things, doubt and scepticism seep in as the original reason for reform becomes less evident. It is now all too clear that, if the comprehensive school is to enjoy a renewal of confidence in public esteem, an attempt to examine what it should be doing, and then to consider how best to do it, is going to be essential.

The assumption of this book is that the comprehensive school should be seen, and increasingly is being seen, as the normal secondary school for all pupils. It follows that if we address ourselves to these fundamental questions, we are involved in discussing education itself. It would therefore be very easy to fill this chapter with selected opinions – some conflicting, others reinforcing – from the considerable number of philosophers, sociologists and psychologists who profess views on what education is about. At the end, it would be yet another 'reader': another set of questions looking for answers. But, of course, everybody has views on education; merely having attended school is generally regarded as a sufficient qualification. And there is a real sense in which education is too important, and too expensive (its budget, in all countries, usually coming next after defence in appropriation) to be left to the educators. Whether we like it or not, education is in the political arena, and politicians are also fairly ready to pronounce on what it should all be about.

However, it is one thing to talk about education, or the educated man, in general; it is another (but not unrelated) thing to talk about it in the context of a particular kind of school system. And since no one is in a position to demonstrate that his view of education is absolutely better than the next man's, it is a matter of putting forward a set of arguments which can be justified in terms of a particular point of view. It is then for the reader to judge the usefulness of the point of view, and the quality of the argument. A corollary of this is that today's defensible thesis may be tomorrow's abandoned position; important factors will be social, economic and cultural, and they will change. All the same, there is much to be said for trying to establish some purpose, and the lineaments of a structure, for the comprehensive school that can command a reasonable degree of acceptance. Then, in the medium term, one can expect a stable climate of opinion, since what is going on in schools is less a matter of penetrating the unknown; one can make more efficient use of resources at a time when they are bound to be scarce; and harness the improved morale of teachers who are investing in a foreseeable future. Within such a pattern of purpose and structure, though, there is all the room in the world for the idiosyncratic adjustment and response of individual schools; indeed, any framework which failed to allow for, indeed encourage, the school's own participation (such as a nationally imposed curriculum) would be denied any sort of consensus from the start.

And while we can only regret that the comprehensive school's growth came about by political expedient rather than educational design, it would, at the same time, be unrealistic to imagine that if such a design originally existed, it would be unchanged today. Developing a school system from scratch cannot be done from blueprints. It is not a matter of commissioning industrial plant that will function by means of predetermined interactions and conditions, and meet established norms. Schools, and the process of education, draw upon so many diverse talents and skills, and give rise to unpredictable and unquantifiable effects. There are many outside influences, and public acceptability will depend on many kinds of assessment. The analogy is rather with the development of some new technological species of artefact, related to public taste and subject in the same way to a variety of contributions and disciplines. The motor car, for example, first took shape as an adaptation of what was already there – a carriage with horses. So it started life as an additive combination of carriage and engine, each recognisable as a distinct part, much as the grammar school and modern school have been added together under one roof to make the horseless-carriage type of comprehensive. There is then a period of development, when the contributory fields of technique or inquiry become integrated with the new invention in its own right. At this stage extreme solutions emerge, which may be basically unworkable or simply ahead of their time. Thus Lanchester's automatic transmission, or the steam car, may be paralleled by schools based on inter-disciplinary inquiry, or on participation, as overarching aims. But finally the new technology finds itself, and by 1914 cars had begun to look like cars; thereafter the basic design structure has hardly changed, as we can see from the report in *Motor* (29.9.76) welcoming the new Ford Cortina: 'There is plenty of life yet in the traditional 3-box car with a front engine driving the back wheel through a live axle . . . excellent results can still be obtained through evolution rather than revolution, by *the continuous development and refinement of a basically simple concept*' (my italics).

The point of this analogy is to suggest that the comprehensive school is coming to the end of its first exploratory period, and that we can now think more clearly about what it is in business to do, and use existing technology to put together a 'basically simple concept' which is *sui generis* a recognisable vehicle for comprehensive education. Then we can look forward to a process of development and refinement, when individual schools can tune up to give the best response to their own needs and constraints by a process of continuous product improvement – that is, of school-based curriculum change. This does not mean that all schools will be the same, any more than all motor cars are the same. It means simply that we shall know what we are supposed to be doing, and have a very good idea of how to do it.

The idea of a common school attended by all children in a district is plainly an egalitarian one. Thus Richard Cobden in1854:

> Notwithstanding the great gulf that separates the middle from the working classes, and the middle from the higher classes in this country, nothing would tend so much to break down that barrier as to erect common schools of so superior a quality that people should find nowhere in their vicinity an opportunity – whatever the class might be – of giving the children a better opportunity than by availing themselves of the facilities afforded by the common schools.

The same radical wish was expressed by Tawney in 1943:

> The England of the next twenty years will not be a nest of singing birds. Those who guide the nation's schools can do more than is given to most men to create the common culture which at present we lack. To serve educational needs, without regard to the vulgar irrelevancies of class and income, is part of the teacher's honour.

What perhaps makes Cobden's voice the more realistic is his recognition that not any old common school will do: it has to be the best thing going. What makes Tawney's more valuable is his linking of the common school with a common culture. The proposition is surely this: something is offered in a common school which is worth having for its own sake, and which is presented in a unifying way so as to bring pupils together rather than separate them. This could be called a cohesive view. On the one hand, it finds common ground with philosophers of education who argue that education is a good in itself; on the other, it marks out, in its emphasis on bringing classes together, political ground which now lies in the centre of the party debate, and at the same time it promotes the social unity which so many studies have shown to be desirable.

But there is another way of viewing the comprehensive principle. Sidney Webb wrote in 1908: 'What we have learned, gradually and slowly, is that nothing worthy of the name of a national system of education can be built up out of a single undifferentiated type, however numerous and however excellent they may be.' What was needed was 'the progressive differentiation of the publicly provided school – the "Common school" of our radical grandfathers – into a number of specialised schools each more accurately fitting the needs of a particular section of children.' This is a differentiating view, and if it is to be applied to a single school, it implies a 'multilateral', one that provides a range of courses of study. The planner, as education officer to the LCC, of London's post-war comprehensives, Sir Graham Savage, has said: 'everyone was calling these schools multilateral then, and I thought that was an awful name. I said "comprehensive", for two reasons: one, because they will cater for every activity; two, because all children from a given area, regardless of ability, will go to them.'

The argument here is that a comprehensive school will meet the needs of its pupils not by introducing them to a set of common experiences, but by fitting them to a sufficient variety of courses, or curricula, or activities. It has been a remarkably pervasive view and bears closer examination. The key thing is that it takes its starting point from the differences between pupils, rather than a desire to unite them. Nowadays, too, we twitch at Webb's use of the word 'needs'; it reinforces the feeling that here is the good socialist, ensuring that children can rise through the system by providing opportunities to match their abilities. It is a view of education that can easily be used to justify a tripartite system. Simon (1974) writes:

> Another kind of study is required to determine why 'Board doctrine' had such staying power, when the conditions to throw it overboard existed. It prevailed throughout the period of the first post-war Labour government.

But if it is seen as a doctrine for a meritocratic system, it looks quite respectable and well-intentioned. It can be used, too, to justify a school curriculum which aims at variety of courses and subjects, because in that way the more opportunities exist to promote individual choice and thus promote a greater development of talent. So here it is again, being deployed by an advocate of comprehensive education on behalf of fourth- and fifth-year multiple-choice schemes (Benn, 1971):

> This kind of 13 plus timetable, continued up through the fifth year, permits a school to maintain a common educational experience for all pupils, and to eliminate course segregation, while at the same time permitting individualisation of programmes as pupils move towards leaving age. . . . It is rapidly becoming the most popular pattern in Britain's comprehensive schools.

This quotation shows how the two different views – the cohesive and the differentiating – can become confused. Because the one thing which multiple-option schemes certainly don't do is maintain a common educational experience. It is worth adding, too, that the individualisation they are designed to promote may be a matter more of appearance than reality. It is surprising how little real variety of programme such systems generate, when all the logistic difficulties in a particular school have been met.

The disadvantages of this 'equality of opportunity' view of comprehensive education have been pointed out by Daunt (1975). He suggests rather that the guiding principle should be that the education of all children is held to be intrinsically of equal value. As a general principle of practice this seems a helpful enough guide, but as an overarching aim it suffers from the disadvantage that it could, perversely, be used to justify a bipartite system by claiming that pupils meeting certain objective-test outcomes need a grammar-school education. I am not convinced by Daunt's refutation of this objection. I would prefer to think that we have no need of this principle; the notion of a common school offering a unified common culture is at once both simpler and capable of different interpretations to meet different constraints. It also makes better political sense than the 'equal value' view, because it is a more accessible idea, and one with strong historical roots.

There is no doubt, though, that the prevailing principle, both administratively and politically, in the development of comprehensive schooling in Britain has up to now been the differentiating, equal-opportunity view. The emphasis in the 1944 Education Act on secondary provision according to the ability and aptitude of pupils can be taken to support this view, just as it has been taken to support parental choice not only between schools, but within them. It is, indeed, a presently fashionable doctrine of consumerism to press for parental influence on the curriculum on these grounds. Thus Michael Young, chairman of the National Consumer Council, as reported in *The Times* of 13 July 1976: 'many parents and pupils do not have a wide choice of schools: their main concern then is choice within school. . . . If schools were more oriented to provision of an individual nature, some of the knotty problems of opting for one school or other could be avoided.' But I am arguing that it is precisely this overweening concern with individual choice that has distorted our comprehensive schools and over-emphasised a meritocratic process of selection which, in a well-known earlier work, Young was at pains to censure. How far, though, this is a fair interpretation of the 1944 Act has recently been questioned by Lord Alexander (in *Education*, 22 October 1976): 'What I believe has happened is that there has been a misinterpretation of the Act . . . the duty of an authority was to cause children to be educated according to their age, ability and aptitude . . . but it was not the intention that the three As should replace the three Rs.' He goes on to argue that the notion of a common core curriculum (in the admittedly limiting context of basic literacy and numeracy skills) was very explicit in the Acts before 1944.

But support for a differentiated curriculum comes from several directions. The Schools Council has always fostered it. Writing of the Council's future in the light of the current debate, the same issue of *Education* observes: 'The whole concept of the "core curriculum" is contrary to the principle of teacher autonomy promulgated in the Report on the Whole Curriculum'. The Council's membership is dominated by teacher organisations, and the suggestion seems to be that the common curriculum threatens the diversity of teacher specialisms. I shall argue later that for a broadly conceived common culture curriculum the very reverse is the case. Again, the Comprehensive Schools Committee, which exists solely to further the schools' interests, has this to say, in a 1976 pamphlet for parents, in answer to the question 'What are the advantages of comprehensive schools?':

Ideals and Possibilities:

> Comprehensive schools get rid of selection. Children are no longer labelled a 'success' or 'failure' at 11 or 12.
> Comprehensive schools offer children a greater variety of courses, subjects and educational opportunities.
> Every child can stay on at school after the leaving age. . . .
> In many areas comprehensive schools make better use of scarce resources.

The first justification is a harking-back to the old, negative 11-plus argument. The second is a lucid statement of the differentiating principle which, I believe, has led directly to our present difficulties. The third is by no means generally true: I know personally of several comprehensives without 'open' sixth-forms. And the last is based on economic, not educational grounds. We shall have to do better than this.

Before we leave the differentiating principle behind, though, it is worth mentioning that it attracts support from some academic sources. Bantock's (1971) argument that a curriculum based on a liberal, humanistic culture is too demanding a diet for the less-able pupils, and that a divided curriculum is required, is well known and has been dealt with by a number of writers (e.g., Lawton, 1975). The only point I need make is that, however unpalatable such a view may seem, it is a perfectly defensible way of presenting the differentiating/equal-opportunity argument. Indeed, precisely because it is logically and closely argued, it serves to show how unsatisfactory a basis that view affords. A more insidious way of attacking the notion of a common curriculum is to advance a *laissez-aller* view of school practice. This is a stance which seems to owe something to the old grammar-school 'rigour in depth' kind of reasoning. Thus Judge (1976):

> From such tangled roots grows the presently flourishing doctrine of the common curriculum . . . against such powerful tendencies towards uniformity should be set the wisdom of pursuing difference. . . . Pupils at the age of 14 often have a not unsatisfactory notion at least of the activities and subjects they wish to pursue.

It is perhaps not a very convincing argument, but it can be subtly influential and needs to be faced: in its near-nihilism, it opens the door either to a very narrow, or indeed to a free-for-all curriculum at 14-plus. It has been effectively tackled, in a different form, by Hirst (1969):

> We have allowed, or rather have insisted on (in the traditional grammar school curriculum) the dropping of subjects from an early age, trusting to the forces of interest, ability and vocational intention to do a responsible selection job for us. But unfortunately the narrow-minded boffin reared on a restricted diet of science and mathematics from 14 or 15, is now all too common a phenomenon, as also is the arts man, blank in his incomprehension of the scientific outlook. . . . You will recall the Crowther Report's fantastic contention that our most able children . . . just do by nature undergo a period of specialist subject-mindedness in their later teens.

I have attempted to show that the notion that the comprehensive school should be guided by a differentiating/equal-opportunity principle has had great influence, and has much to answer for. We can trace to it not only those unsatisfactory aspects of present practice discussed in the first chapter, but also a fragmented, subject-centred approach to curriculum research and development. And because it puts nothing positive in place of the divided grammar/secondary modern curriculum paradigms so evident in our comprehensive schools, it has tended to support a debate conducted all too often in terms of fashionable dichotomies: classical versus romantic; or subject versus child-centred; or open versus closed; or the product versus the process. Much of this has been tiresome and unhelpful. But I believe the proposition that so much of our present disaffections can be traced to this principle has not been generally perceived and I have therefore tried to look at its many forms with some care.

I suggest that in its place we take as our guiding principle the inclusive, coherent principle of initiating all our pupils, during the years of compulsory schooling, into worthwhile aspects of a common culture. After reviewing the extent of support for such a view, I shall suggest the form of structure needed to implement it in the comprehensive school.

A convenient starting point is Oakeshott's view of 'School' as a place where a conscious transaction occurs between generations (1972): 'The idea "School" is . . . that of a serious and orderly initiation into an intellectual, imaginative, moral and emotional inheritance; an initiation designed for children who are ready to embark upon it.' A human being is the inhabitant 'of a world composed, not of "things", but of meanings; that is, of occurrences . . . recognized, identified, understood and responded to in terms of this understanding. . . . To be without this understanding is to be . . . a stranger to the human condition.' A similar point has been made by Peters (1973):

> education consists essentially in the initiation of others into a public world picked out by the language and concepts of a people and structured by rules governing their purposes and interactions with each other. . . . (The teacher's) function is rather to act as a guide in helping them to explore and *share* a public world whose contours have been marked out by generations which have preceded both of them.

In short, we have the idea of education as an intentional, inclusive process concerned primarily with the transmission to pupils of a selection from the culture.

To say that this implies a common curriculum is to beg the questions: How can the selection be made? And how is all this to be implemented? Before passing to those, however, it is worth noting that there is a wide base of political support for the idea of a common curriculum. And there is certainly little point in advancing attractive academic proposals which are simply out of line with political reflections of public opinion, and cannot command support. But there are different interpretations to be put upon the term 'the common curriculum', and if this is taken to mean a shopping list of subjects jotted down by a headmaster, or politician, or chief education officer, then it is no advance on free-for-all option schemes and just as poor a substitute for curriculum planning. There are others who take a common curriculum to be a nationally imposed compulsory curriculum; and although White (1973) has argued an ingenious theoretical basis for such a programme, the proposal runs counter to the English tradition of an education service that is centrally supported and locally administered.

But a curriculum which offers common elements of the culture to all pupils in a school, where the school itself interprets the selection from the culture and the modes of implementation so as to make the most effective use of all its resources, can respond both to national guidelines and also to the local conditions and community. It seems likely that it is this interpretation that will gain the support of the present Labour administration, for the Education and Science Green Paper (July 1977) states:

> This does not presuppose uniform answers: schools, pupils, and their teachers are different and the curriculum should be flexible enough to reflect these differences. But there is a need to investigate the part which might be played by a 'protected' or 'core' element of the curriculum common to all schools.

This is a view which would seem to lie in the central ground politically. For example, the Conservative MP Timothy Raison has written (*The Times*, 20 February 1973):

> My conviction is that comprehensive schools must be committed to the transmission of our traditional culture and academic values, though certainly in a searching and fresh rather than a stereotyped way. . . . When it comes to the point it will not only be middle-class parents who take that view. There has always been a strong and admirable commitment among many working-class people that they, too, want the best. . . . Moreover, at its extreme there can be something halfway between insulting and defeatist in the idea of providing a different sort of culture for the workers. Of course the style in which our civilization and crafts should be conveyed to different children must vary with their circumstances. But the essence should be the same.

I quote this at some length because Raison not only makes a clear stand for a common culture curriculum; he advocates it for its own sake, rather than its instrumental value, and takes an effective side-swipe at the bipartite approach into the bargain.

How, then, do we identify 'the essence'? Lawton (1975) stresses the two important aspects of coverage and balance: 'no important area should be missed out from our selection from the culture, but also the question of balance is very important.' He goes on to advocate thinking in terms of disciplines or faculties rather than subject departments and advances a detailed scheme. Whitfield (1973) has a slightly different emphasis. He suggests the three sources which might act as a focus for planning the secondary curriculum are society, the individual pupil, and man's acquired knowledge and understanding. He argues that if we are searching for 'a fundamental referent' for curriculum planning, only the third 'stands as an irreducible element, for both our sense of community and our ideal of the person are contingent upon this aspect'. The other two aspects he sees as logically of secondary importance.

Whitfield goes on to suggest that 'the two most helpful and scholarly analyses available to us for curricular purposes are, I believe, P.H. Hirst's seven "forms of knowledge" and P.H. Phenix's six "realms of meaning".' He then devises a programme using Phenix as a basis. Another interesting view comes from Skilbeck (1972). He sees programmes for the systematic study of discrete intellectual disciplines as based on 'a model of human action of which rationality in the form of reflective, intentional behaviour is the central feature.' He contrasts this analytic approach with a synthetic one, which would 'explore a core curriculum built around the major categories of cultural action. These include language, myth and belief systems, patterns of political institutions, work cultures, child-rearing and education, the maintenance of social order, the arts and scientific culture.' He concedes that both analytic and synthetic approaches 'share an interest in wholeness', in the sense of educating the whole child; and concludes that 'despite the difficulties, there are arguments in favour of a core curriculum centred in the analysis of these and similar categories of action. . .'. The kind of cultural map or synthetic approach advocated here by Skilbeck has been advanced by Broudy, Smith and Burnett (1965).

Education is a complex field of inquiry, and it can hardly come as a surprise to see that the detailed implementation of a common curriculum will involve difficult choices. The nature of these will be examined in the next chapter. In particular, the process of curriculum design will be associated with a deliberative process in each individual school. The important thing for the moment is not the rich diversity of interpretations of the coherent principle of the common curriculum, but rather the clarity and universality which attend the notion of a core curriculum that reveals the unity and order of our culture. Enough has been said to show that two dangers exist: at the one extreme, there is a risk that the sheer volume of material may lead to an unbalanced selection, with two much emphasis on particular aspects of our culture. It will not be enough to base choice on mere compromise; however elusive and arguable, the concept of balance may need some formal mode of expression. At the other extreme, there is a risk that the common core will be seen in narrow terms, like C.P. Snow's simplistic arts-and-science two cultures. Even worse, the common core may be advocated simply because it offers a secure basis for education that is merely useful.

Since this is a stance which has not been absent from the present debate on secondary education, it is vital that schools know where they stand. Oakeshott (1972) sees this argument as particularly harmful:

> It is to be recognised as a frustration of the educational engagement and a destruction of 'School' because it attributes to the teaching and learning which comprise this apprenticeship an extrinsic 'end' or 'purpose'; namely, the integration of the newcomer into a current 'society' recognised as the manifold of skills, activities, enterprises, understandings, sentiments and beliefs required to keep it going; in short, to rear the most 'current' men possible.

The weakness in setting schools to rear the most 'current' men and women is that the skills which appear so much in demand today may be at a discount tomorrow. Paradoxically, then, the right way to educate pupils to flourish in an adaptive, fluid, multivalent society is to give them that personal autonomy which can only come from a broadly based education; an education which in its theoretical intentions deliberately eschews aims that are useful in the current, vernacular sense. It goes without saying that such an education would see instruction in the 'three Rs' as a necessary part of its tasks; but hardly a sufficient one. And because such a programme would be concerned with the development of mind, fatuous behavioural distinctions between the cognitive and affective domains would have no place in it. For when a pupil is led to show understanding for others, and of his own part in his relations with others, he is acquiring cognitive knowledge. It is then possible to get a fresh perspective on 'pastoral care', and ensure that the school's real priorities centre in the widest sense on its pupils' intellectual growth.

But a common curriculum, based on a concept of liberal education, will not form the totality of a school's programme. As Hirst observes (1965): 'Liberal education as is here being understood is only one part of the education a person ought to have, for it omits quite deliberately for instance specialist education, physical education and character training.' Although we can, and in my view should, keep instrumental aims out of our common core considerations, we must recognise that it would be an odd sort of comprehensive school where there were no games, where the teachers took no interest in whether or not the pupils were polite, or where the pupil with an artistic or scientific or practical bent could not pursue these inclinations by making an individual choice. In short, schools must to an extent respond to the personal skills of pupils, and to the instrumental tasks placed on them in certain ways by society. Important among the latter are physical education and the learning of foreign languages as a basic competence; for attempts to justify these curriculum elements as distinct forms of knowledge and understanding are unconvincing. Indeed, in some respects it would be helpful to schools if the Department of Education and Science were to acknowledge this as a curriculum area for national decision-making. Linguists frequently lament the extent to which French has almost entirely displaced German, and become the first foreign language in most schools; while others argue for Chinese, Russian or Spanish to replace German as a second. A clear policy, possibly introducing different priorities in different areas, would prevent waste and ensure cultural continuity in the modern languages field. But I stress that the justification for such a step would be the instrumental nature of the curriculum elements involved; there is no suggestion here that the common curriculum, as liberal education, should be determined nationally.

While, therefore, a proportion of the resources of the school will, over the five years of compulsory schooling, advance diverse personal skills and some vocational and instrumental aims, the bulk of the school's effort will be concentrated on a substantial common core which will aim to equip pupils for the life of learning that lies ahead. It is a non-instrumental aim, since it seeks to promote understanding for its own sake; but it has nothing to do with inert knowledge and sees education, as Whitehead put it, as 'the acquisition of the art of the utilisation of knowledge'. It is by no means a new view of education, and because a liberal education leads directly to individual autonomy, it ought to leave students in the condition of continually asking questions. Another way of making the same point is to be found in the Unesco study, *Learning to Be* (1972): lifelong education will help man 'find his path through reality towards the ideal of the complete man'. And again the aims of an educational system are seen in broad terms:

> We see these universally valid aims in scientific humanism; in the development of reason; in creativity; in the spirit of social responsibility; in the search for balance among the various intellectual, ethical, emotional and physical components of personality and in a positive perception of mankind's historic fate.

The task now is to see what sort of structure, in general rather than in detail, the curriculum of a comprehensive school might have to implement a programme along these lines. Given that the curriculum is not an elastic bag but tightly confined to about 1,500 minutes weekly of contact time as lessons, and that the problem with a common culture curriculum is what to leave out rather than what to put in, it makes sense to start by seeing how much time cannot be allocated to the common curriculum. While the common core will be seen as a five-year continuum, the fact that 16-plus exam syllabuses are conceived as two-year programmes in practical terms is bound to mean a discreet change of gear in years 4 and 5. In any case, somewhere between year 1 and year 5 pupils acquire a maturer view of themselves and an idea of how society views them. Year 3 is frequently the pivot for this kind of realisation, and it follows that some sort of option device offering choices in personal skills and individual talents will be needed for years 4 and 5. There is no harm in seeing these in subject terms, and perhaps some convenience in it as far as CSE and O-level examinations go. It is generally accepted that approximately four 35-minute periods, or their equivalent, are sufficient weekly in years 4 and 5 for an examination subject, and this is about 10 per cent of the total time available. What needs will arise? Consider first the extent to which pupils may want to extend provision already made in the common core. The chief claimant here is likely to be science. It is reasonable to suppose that its common core component will be sufficient to take all pupils to a single 16-plus pass, but no more. And it is possible for the needs of potential science sixth-formers to be met by a two-subject certification (e.g., Schools Council Integrated Science Project). It follows that one option column will be needed to provide the one extra science allocation for interested pupils.

There is next the question of foreign languages. If they lie, as I have suggested they should, outside the compulsory common core, then at least one other option column will be needed to allow the double science choice to be taken with one foreign language. It might be argued that a third option column is needed, to meet the needs of those requiring a second foreign language as well. Certainly, though, no more than three columns, corresponding to 30 per cent option time, will be needed; because alongside the science and languages there will be plenty of room to insert personal skill subjects in the areas of art and craft, business and engineering studies and so on. (Bear in mind that the common core will, on any reading, include studies in the aesthetic/creative domain.) I shall suggest in Chapter 3 that two option columns are sufficient.

It might now be supposed that in years 1 to 3 all the time can be devoted to the common curriculum, along with an allocation for the first foreign language and physical activities. It has been assumed, by the way, that the non-optional element in years 4 and 5 includes physical activities. For if these are seen instrumentally, as aspects of health education and a preparation for the use of leisure, then it seems illogical and unreasonable that they should be optional when pupils are reaching physical maturity. But this is bound to reflect the culture of a particular society; it would be an unthinkable proposition, no doubt, in France.

The only difficulty arises in years 1 to 3 with the second foreign language. A draconian solution is to have none of it till the fourth year options, but this is open to the serious objection that its choice would be based on non-existent knowledge and at a late stage in the game. But to allocate as much as 10 per cent of the time to yet another foreign language in the second or third year, at the expense of the common curriculum in perhaps its most demanding phase, seems hard to justify. In any case, it will not be offered, as will the first foreign language, to all pupils; for while that step seems justified on grounds of equal access before making the choice in year 4, it hardly seems to stretch to a second language. So an option device will be needed. The answer to this difficulty is bound to be a compromise, just as it is with first-generation comprehensives. Possibly a second-language introductory option, open to all and taking up about 5 per cent of the time in the third year, is the right sort of answer.

The pattern of the curriculum for the first five years is now taking some shape. In years 1 and 2, all will follow the same course; a common culture curriculum, along with a foreign language and physical activities. In year 3, the only variation will be the introduction, at the expense of the common core, of an additional option promoting a second language choice. In years 4 and 5 the common core, and physical activities, continue; but there are two, perhaps three option choices to meet a range of individual needs.

This is a very different pattern, particularly in years 4 and 5, from that currently found in comprehensives. And nothing has yet been said about how it can be made to work across the whole ability range. In place of the usual extrinsic choice between subjects for 80 per cent of fourth- and fifth- year time, there is a mandatory common curriculum. In later chapters I shall deal with these questions of structure, pedagogy and organisation. But it is not difficult to see the lines along which we shall proceed. It is reasonably clear that the selection from the culture that forms the basis of the common curriculum will not in general work in terms of separate subjects all along the line. The case will be strong for the establishment of faculties, which may well preserve subject conceptual structures, or even be based on a single subject domain; but their task will be to present key aspects of the culture in ways which, enterprisingly yet honestly, can be said to initiate all pupils into them. It is at once evident that this is the real meaning of choice. It is taken for granted that pupils will come to see what has to be transacted in many different ways – that their kinds of understanding, and capacities for understanding, will need a variety of different learning strategies. So the essence of the design will be not extrinsic choice between subjects, but intrinsic choice between approaches to the same unifying theme.

Another implication follows from this, which marks out further the quite different thinking which must underlie this new kind of comprehensive school. For it will no longer be possible for teachers to work in the isolation of their own subject cubicles and private practices. If this kind of richness is to be devised around the cultural aspects seen by each faculty as its programme of learning tasks and desirable outcomes, then the strength and invention that come from teachers working together will be a prerequisite. By the same token, there will be a need for a resource facility; not for its own sake, as a prestige acquisition, and not as a device to promote individualised learning. For that will be only one of the ways in which pupils learn, and to emphasise it at the expense of others is to advance the kind of partial solution which has plagued curriculum reform over the last ten years.

We can see one final implication. We may have our staff working productively in teams, as well as individually; we may have a variety of learning strategies, a clear idea of what we would like to achieve, and a battery of resources to help us. But what can still be missing is easy access by pupils to all these good things. Access, that is, for all pupils; access which is not based on reach-me-down primary school assessments, or on performance at the kinds of things written examinations are designed to test. It must be access that offers each pupil the chance to get the best sort of treatment; and it must take account of the fact that pupils change, and for the better, if all our time and trouble is to make educational sense. The implication is clear. Only a non-streamed format can offer the opportunities an ambitious common culture programme needs if it is to succeed with all pupils. This aspect will be discussed in detail in Chapter 4.

The concept of the common school, then, leads to a curriculum structure for the comprehensive school which is at once both very different from and very much simpler than the stifling and needlessly complicated pattern of ability bands and subject options which so many schools have been led to either by accident, or by what I suggest is a false view of the purpose of comprehensive education. Instead of trying to fit pupils into a differentiating school organisation, we have an inclusive, coherent design which, beneath its outward simplicity, can develop an infrastructure that is flexible enough to fit the responses of each child.

Chapter 3

Value Judgments and Curriculum Design

The argument so far has led to the suggestion that a curriculum which aims to induct all pupils into a common culture would give the comprehensive school the educational rationale which it at present lacks. Present practice is derived from an attempt to assimilate the differing patterns and procedures of the grammar and modern schools, thus provoking an uncertainty of intention which can seriously impair the effectiveness of any institution. And while curriculum theory seems abundant, it is rich in points of view, rather than in insights that can be located in and related to the practice of education. Perhaps this would not matter if there were clarity about the educational purpose of the comprehensive school; but its original rationale was political and social, and a lingering obsession with its function as a differentiating rather than unifying institution has obscured the need to think hard about what such schools are for.

Yet, once we return to the notion of the common school, we can postulate a purpose which can achieve a remarkably wide consensus of support. Furthermore, it is a purpose which suggests a curriculum structure, and I have given it an outline in the last chapter. We need now to look at this structure in greater detail, and see how it can frame the moving pictures of curriculum process. But in shifting our focus from the general design to its separate components, we must be careful not to fall into a trap which awaits all who see curriculum design, development and implementation as a primrose path between distinct stages. Because, in a school, the teacher in the classroom must have as clear a view of the course ahead as anyone else; neither is the process of education a linear path which can be charted and checked as part of a grand design. Yet it is not without structure, and must indeed be regarded as an intentional process, with certain accepted product criteria. The paradox goes like this: if we specify, we not only restrict, we may make distinctions between content and method, design and implementation and so on which are ultimately unsound; while if we are content to assume that statements of general aims, or criteria, or *aide-memoire* objectives will alone ensure satisfactory classroom experiences, we may be in for a nasty shock.

The way out of this is to hold on tight to a view of the school as a whole. If we allow a theoretic paradigm to dominate, we may become stuck in the mire of a philosopher's attempts to tidy up the structure of knowledge, or a sociologist's attempts to ensure that each pupil is reifying concepts so as to construct his own reality; and rebound towards a philistine view of school as a bureaucratic operation where smooth decision-making and systematic delegation sweep all before them. Subject specialisms, too will colour each teacher's picture of the design and it must be part of a school's own educative function to extend his vision. Whitehead's remark that the problem of education is to make the pupil see the wood by means of the trees is as true for the staff of a school. Unless the working-out of a curriculum takes account of the everyday realities and constraints in the individual school, while preserving a holistic view of what it is hoped to achieve, there will be a lack of engagement and effectiveness.

Just how important these attributes are to innovation emerges from a massive government study of 30,000 pupils in American schools, published recently by the American Institute for Research. It has concluded that many of the innovations introduced over the last 20 years – including team teaching, open classrooms, moveable timetables, teacher aides and individualised instruction – make very little difference to pupils' achievement. The researchers offered some possible explanations: pupils' loss of self-motivation, teachers' lack of involvement, inappropriate matches between educational approaches and pupils' needs, and the insensitivity of standard measurements to new ideas and practices. But the overall conclusion is clear: 'Educational quality is *not* synonymous with innovation or individualisation.'

It is clear from our own experience that curriculum innovation is so often seen by schools as a cosmetic improvement to separate parts rather than a basic change in the whole. Writing of the 38 schools involved in the Schools Council Keele Integrated Studies Project between 1968 and 1971, Shipman (1974) writes: 'Never in the schools studied here was there any attempt to see a project or a combination of projects, whether initiated by the Schools Council or local advisers, as involving the whole school in planned change involving all the staff.' Unless innovation is locked into the school's whole strategy, it is bound to make little difference in the long run.

But it is all too easy for sectional interests to confine innovation to separate segments; and these interests may extend beyond teaching staff to advisers, community pressure groups and governors. Yet unless a sufficient consensus is sustained in developing the broad strategies into the detail of curriculum, that essential coherence will be lost. It is clear, then, we need not be worried about getting some answers; what matters above all is asking the right questions, or (which comes to the same thing) making changes for the right reasons. For example, to embark upon a non-streamed organisation in order to promote purely social goals is to invite confusion and resentment among staff, and probably among pupils and parents as well. But to do so because it will increase curriculum effectiveness is not only to justify it in educational terms; it is also to give the change some chance of outlasting transitory enthusiasms, and see it as part of a coherent plan.

The first task, therefore, must be to interpret the idea of a common culture curriculum in ways which are likely both to command consensus and promote understanding. These first steps are the most important, because an initial deviation can lead one profoundly off course, and this can be confusing and expensive when a five-year plan is being laid. And they are not easy; the recent interim study (1975) by the Group for Research and Innovation in Higher Education noted that 'developing a new idea and implementing it is not a simple matter, even within a single institution.' If the new programme is to succeed within both school and community, and thus hit the bedrock of wide political support, three attributes would seem to be necessary:

1 The basic idea must find sympathy with what Ernest Bevin called 'the horse sense of the common people'. There is no reason why this restricts us to a strategy of drifting with the tide, or of preserving what is already there; but it rules out those which will gain only fringe support.
2 The programme must be based on a coherent, underpinning and self-consistent view of education, to which staff can return to clarify their thoughts and procedures. This will be not an ironclad doctrine to be pursued at all costs, but rather a reasoned support system to steer by when the going is uncertain.
3 The scheme must have the cardinal virtue of simplicity. If there is one quality which promotes flexible solutions, minimises misunderstandings and gives an open-weave texture to the curriculum fabric, it is the simplicity which avoids complex qualification and categorisation in its initial presentation. Then there is scope for adaptation and re-interpretation as the nexus of argument moves to questions of choice and action.

Let us look at possible interpretations of the common curriculum in the light of these considerations. There is first the suggestion, which has been made frequently by apologists for the present system of late, that existing comprehensive schools do in effect operate a common curriculum in all but name. It is true that multiple-option schemes are often manipulated so as to cover a range of subjects: to ensure that at least one science is taken, for example. But not only does this increase the logistic complexity of an already complicated system; simply to make sure a pupil is 'doing physics' is quite different from initiating him into the nature of scientific understanding. As Hirst (1969) has put it, 'our eyes have been far too fixed on the specialist training of the young physicist to find out what is needed in courses in physics that will develop a sympathetic grasp of the cognitive structure of science, an appreciation of what it involves and therefore a recognition of its significance in the rational life.' It is interesting to note that the same point has been made more recently (Jenkins, 1976) by a lecturer in science education: 'The production of qualified chemists is not the function of secondary schools . . . the proposal for a common system of examination at 16 plus . . . means reassessing the contribution chemistry can make to general education.'

Putting strings on subject-option schemes misses the point of the common curriculum as an initiating cultural experience, and can bring pupils nowhere near to it. In schools, the labels may mean nothing much; it is what happens in the classroom that matters, and that is why original intentions matter. Here there is no coherent view of education, and tremendous timetable complexity. On two of the three counts suggested, this interpretation of a common curriculum fails.

Before taking our own ideas further there are one or two other variations that are worth mentioning. I have in mind first a school which has made a significant move from the traditional multiple-option pattern to one which reduces fourth- and fifth-year options to two columns (that is, two sets of subject choices), alongside faculties in creative studies (art, craft and music); English; European studies (European studies, French and German); mathematics; science (separate subjects and integrated science) and social studies (geography, history, religious education). But in the first two years, English and social studies are combined in a programme called Enquiry. This is certainly a step in the right direction, but really goes only half-way as it stands. Uncertainty about the role of English, compounded by a rigid separation of geography from history in social studies (in spite of its name), means a lack of continuity between 'Enquiry' in the first two years and an essentially subject-dominated approach in the remaining three. The difficulty with European studies comes in the fourth and fifth years. For one thing, it is necessary to distinguish a top set, who are being taught European history and geography in French; another who are taught these subjects in English; and a bottom set for whom any foreign language teaching means problems. But there are more important objections. How skilled are modern languages teachers likely to be in handling, say, the historical concepts arising from the discussion of the Spanish civil war? Is it satisfactory to argue that the aim of the course is simply breadth, not depth? And what, in any case, are the aims of teaching languages in this way? Are they the same for all pupils?

Plainly there are difficulties in moving to a thorough-going common curriculum in one step. But it is arguable that, providing care is taken to ensure that in the initial planning for change due attention is paid to the need for a close look at underlying philosophical issues to do with the nature of knowledge, and the need to keep the basic lines simple, then later confusion can be avoided. It is interesting to compare this scheme – the result of curriculum development in an established school – with one that has been launched in a new comprehensive: the Stantonbury campus at Milton Keynes. There are three compulsory areas with continuity over five years; creative studies once again, along with mathematics and science. And a foreign language is compulsory in the first two years. The rest of the curriculum is given over to a compulsory area of interdisciplinary studies, and a free-choice component which includes one day a fortnight devoted to a free choice of personal hobbies and interests, and a subject-option element in the fourth and fifth years. But the compulsory interdisciplinary area also involves choice, arising out of a thematically based structure geared to an extensive resource centre.

This looks like a well-meaning attempt to please everyone which could well end up pleasing no one. As a result there is needless complication; ten-day timetables simply double the work for a start. And why make creative studies compulsory, while leaving history and English to fend for themselves in an area where the conceptual structures of disciplines seem blurred? And given the difficulty of squeezing into the curriculum all the planned experiences we can see are worthwhile, it seems difficult to justify a hobbies-based sector other than in extra-curricular time. Once again, what appears to be lacking is a clearly understood unifying view of the school's educational purpose.

It is doubtful, indeed, whether a proposal to devote 10 per cent of curriculum time to hobbies would get off the ground in many areas of the country without riding roughshod over the feelings of parents and governors. But there need be no misgivings in seeking support for a common curriculum which presents a coherent educational strategy, even though such a scheme is unusual and represents a break with tradition. It does, however, mean that the school must be prepared to educate both pupils and parents. At the beginning, parents' support is assured if the three preconditions specified can be met. But as time passes and teething troubles are met, parents will need reassurance that all is well in both the short and the long term. And even if an innovatory curriculum is successful, parents may still have to come to terms with the fact that it is different from the schools they knew themselves. They will want to believe that it is right to be different; but they may not easily see how to believe it.

This point has been brought out in an M. Phil. thesis by Williamson (1976), who studied the performance of 23 matched pairs of pupils going to two comprehensive schools in the same area but with different curriculum approaches. School A had reorganised on bilateral lines, preserving the streamed structure of its former constituent grammar and modern schools; School B was non-streamed and implemented a common curriculum. Over a five-year period the pupils were tested in basic subjects, their O-level and CSE results compared, and their attitudes to school climate and further study compared. The attitudes of both teachers and parents were also investigated by questionnaire and interview. The study showed that the schools' different policies had markedly different effects, and that whereas school A imposed limits on students in its curriculum structure, school B offered academic success to a wider range of pupils; its students were more positively in favour of their school; and more wished to stay into the sixth form. But 'school B had difficulties in getting parents to understand its definition of schooling. . . . Parents of school A knew what was going on in the school. . . . In school B, the school was blamed for lack of progress. But in school A, parents accepted the school's definition of their children, and felt lack of progress was their child's fault.'

The re-educative aspect of curriculum change has been given some attention with respect to staff, but its importance for an innovating school's parents has perhaps not been widely noticed. We must recognise that the curriculum which truly reflects the common school will adopt a stance which is quite different from that of the grammar school, because it will take a wider view of culture, validate its judgments in different ways, and introduce different styles of learning. It is in many ways a stance which Skilbeck (1973) has termed reconstructionist:

> This strategy requires schools to relate their activities essentially to three things. First, schools need a set of educational criteria, possibly in the form of objectives, which have been worked through by the school staff and others who can reasonably claim a stake in the process. Second, the schools need to have formed a clear understanding of the effects of what they have done in the past. Third, the schools need to look ahead, anticipating the effects of present trends in culture and relating all of their work explicitly to the assessments they are able to make.

A common culture curriculum should prove to be sensitive and yet demanding in exactly these ways, and therefore assured of support, providing leadership and sensibility are exercised in forming and presenting its design. This is where a recognition in every decision of the school as a whole is such a key factor. For example, it may be argued by staff that if Spanish is the first foreign language, more pupils are likely to achieve success with it than with French because of its easier structures in the early stages. And language teachers tend to support moves which reduce the dominance of French. But with a declining school population, competition between schools in an area will become increasingly important, and my own experience is that many parents, rightly or wrongly, regard Spanish as a soft option. There would then be a risk of abler pupils drifting to nearby schools offering French as the first language. In the last analysis, heads are paid to make judgments based on all these factors, and for this reason alone the inclination to delegate responsibility for curriculum decisions to a subordinate would appear most unwise; or, for that matter, exclusively to a moot, committee or other similar body. A more trivial example, yet one whose effects can be far-reaching, might arise over school uniform. The staff of a school taking a reconstructionist view of curriculum are unlikely to be sympathetic to uniform rules, *per se*; yet parents and governors may have unshakeable, if unprovable, convictions that a school that lacks a uniform lacks discipline. Here again, a head must exercise leadership skills, and convince staff that if parents want uniform (and this can be established by setting up a parent-teacher association committee), then there need be no harm in having it; rather might it bring much good, in that parental support is likely to be more readily forthcoming for a necessary but novel curriculum departure. The problem is then defused as a doctrinaire issue, and becomes the infinitely more tractable one of devising a uniform which reflects the views of parents and pupils and is easy to administer.

I have tried to indicate how my first criterion of commonsense support need not stand in the way of a reforming programme. The matter of defining educational criteria for a common curriculum must be tackled next. It seems important that these are established with some rigour, for it is not difficult to make up shopping-lists when – as at present – there is disquiet about the effects of excessive choice. In this country the DES has so far confined itself to leading questions: 'How would the common core be defined – is it just mathematics and English or does it extend to science, modern languages and further?' And it seems unlikely that the present debate will lead to a single range of answers. But it may well establish a climate in which schools try to work out their own, and if this process is based on collectivist head-counting on the one hand, or *ex cathedra* statements on the other, the result may be a lurch from one kind of muddle to another just as pernicious. Certainly there are signs that a swing to common core prescriptions has begun across the Atlantic. In Ontario, the Ministry of Education will insist from September 1977 that pupils of 15 and 16 must obtain two credits in English, two in mathematics, two in Canadian history or geography and one in science. And a document recently published by the Dean of Harvard identifies six characteristics of a core curriculum:

> An educated person must be able to think and write clearly and effectively . . . have an informed acquaintance with the physical and biological sciences, with the historical and quantitative techniques needed for investigating the workings of modern society, with some of the important scholarly, literary and artistic achievements of the past and with the major religious and philosophical conceptions of man . . . have good manners and high aesthetic and moral standards.

While at San Diego University, the general education programme will have three divisions: basic subjects – English composition, mathematics or logic, and oral communication; foundations of learning – life and physical sciences, social sciences and the humanities; and what is termed the Human Experience, where all credit units have to be earned in courses listed under a single theme.

These changes stem in part from dissatisfaction with the general education of new students after heavily optioned college courses, which arose in the 1960s and were hastened by student activism. Writing in 1971, Eisner listed three 'persistent dilemmas in curriculum decision-making' at an American conference: first, 'the goal of enabling students to formulate their own educational purposes . . . [and] the problem of reconciling it with the ideal of utilizing the best and widest array of knowledge available.' Second, 'the age-old question of how to achieve balance . . . how does one ensure the cultivation of idiosyncracy while, at the same time, requiring students to study the wide range of subject matters that make for educationally balanced men?' And third, '. . . the problem of evaluating the educational consequences of the programs we construct or endorse.' An awareness of these persistent dilemmas is a prerequisite for curriculum planners; and as society's values shift, so the emphasis will move from one judgment to another. This is why a broad base for curriculum deliberation in a school is as important as the need Skilbeck mentions to anticipate trends. In a university context, richer staffing and a research capacity allow these prescriptions for an educated person a wider scope than is possible in a school, where the case for an underpinning rationale is therefore particularly desirable.

Such a rationale will not be a detailed curriculum blueprint. The analogy is perhaps rather with the brief we would give an architect for the essential facilities we would like a new house to offer us. Here, we want not a house but a common school which, in Lawton's words (1975), will '. . . transmit a common culture and provide an adequate means for individual development within the general framework of that culture.' The brief will need to be precise enough to specify those aspects of the culture with which we must be concerned, but capable of a flexible enough interpretation to allow us to adapt it to the particular milieu of staff, students and community. We want to be free, like an architect, to shape the brief to our own needs and style, not least because (unlike an architect) we shall have to live with it. The brief must be complete, but with no redundant information to cloud our judgment; if we depart from it, we will do so knowingly and will know why.

It follows that what we are looking for is not so much a statement of aims and objectives at this stage, but rather a ground plan which will map out for us the way in which we should make our selection from the culture. Lawton has looked at the views of three theorists whose attitudes to culture and education are very different: Bantock, Hirst and Williams. He concludes:

> To a very limited extent all three . . . are in agreement: they all recognise the importance of the transmission of culture as the basis of education, and to some extent they identify the same aspects of our traditional culture as important – for example, art and music. But they also differ considerably in the emphasis they place on certain aspects of our culture and also the kinds of selection they would make as a basis for curriculum planning. . . . There are also other more fundamental differences: Bantock believes in different kinds of curricula for different kinds of cultural groups; Hirst advocates a common curriculum for all, based on a recognition of the importance of forms of knowledge; Williams sees the purposes of a common curriculum as even wider, having social as well as cognitive perspectives. None of them has attempted to describe in detail how a selection from the culture might be made and structured as a planned school curriculum.

Hirst's position is based on a concept of liberal education. He writes (1965):

> Ever since Greek times this idea of education has had its place. Sometimes it has been modified or extended in detail to accommodate within its scheme new forms of knowledge; sometimes the concept has been misinterpreted. . , sometimes it has been strongly opposed on philosophical grounds. . . . Yet at crucial points in the history of education the concept has constantly reappeared . . . There has . . . arisen the demand for an education whose definition

and justification are based on the nature and significance of knowledge itself, and not on the predilections of the pupils, the demands of society, or the whims of politicians.

It is clear that there is a close connection between the idea of a liberal education and that of initiating a pupil into the forms of thought which will give him autonomy, in the sense of making responsible choices about his view of the good life. This is at once a proposal which is capable of analysis by philosophers of education so as to provide a rigorous basis, and an idea which has captured the hearts and minds of men for centuries. It is, as Lawton reminds us, one choice of many we can make; but it is a choice which combines the virtues of coherence and simplicity with the strength and accessibility that can make it the basis for the kind of common-sense agreement I have suggested we shall need. If we can find such an analysis, it will be up to us to develop it into the detail of a structured and planned school curriculum; to harness our social and psychological insights – and our practical intuition – to make it work in the classroom.

The analysis of Phenix (1964) is based on the concept of realms of meaning. Meaning, as he interprets it, seems to have rather a mystical dimension and his division of classes of meaning into the six realms of symbolics, empirics, aesthetics, synnoetics, ethics and synoptics does not seem a particularly accessible one, and is not without some ambiguity. The analysis offered by Hirst (1965) seems altogether more helpful. The differentiated modes in which Hirst (along with other philosophers) suggests mind is developed are termed forms of knowledge and experience, and distinguished as: formal logic and mathematics, the physical sciences, an understanding of our own and other people's minds, moral judgment and awareness, aesthetic experience, religious concepts and philosophical understanding. This list is but the bare bones, and reference to Hirst's widely available paper is essential to see how such a programme could be planned and conducted; and to see that 'understanding a form of knowledge is far more like coming to know a country than climbing a ladder'.

The close reasoning of Hirst's analysis, and its natural historical links with liberal education as a part of our culture (if not of the grammar or modern styles of curriculum) make it a useful basis for our brief. But other expositions may, for one reason or another, appeal more strongly to an innovating school; and new ones will be devised. It would be interesting, for example, to consider one based on a synthetic rather than analytic approach, using categories of cultural action, as suggested by Skilbeck and mentioned in Chapter 2. And the examination of Hirst's ideas will continue, generating new insights and perhaps new worked-out schemes. That of White (1973) has an acknowledged debt to Hirst, but questions the transcendental justification of his thesis. White is led to distinguish between two kinds of activities: those in which the child must engage in order that an understanding of them is logically possible, and those in which some understanding is possible without an engagement. Those in the first category, in which he includes communication, the physical sciences, pure mathematics, art appreciation and philosophy, become compulsory components; those in the second may be curriculum options, and could include speaking a foreign language, games, cookery and painting.

A more recent exercise is that of Barrow (1976), who takes issue with the arguments of both White and Hirst, but acknowledges his debt to them both. As a philosopher of education, he takes a utilitarian stance:

> Utilitarianism, in the sense that I intend, is grounded on the premiss that what matters ideally is a world in which everyone is happy, that is to say a world in which people are not depressed, anxious, alienated . . . or, more generally, miserable. . . . Education should seek to develop individuals in such a way that they are in a position to gain happiness for themselves, while contributing to the happiness of others.

He goes on to propose a curriculum in four stages, which are not defined precisely. But it would appear that in the secondary school the first two years would involve initiation into the natural sciences, mathematics, the fine arts, history, literature and religion; to be followed for three years by 'the continued study of history and literature and the introduction of vocational and social studies – all as compulsory elements'. New subjects like cookery and modern languages become options, as do 'the continued study of such things as mathematics, the fine arts and the natural sciences'. Barrow's final stage adds philosophy to the compulsory list.

It is interesting to remark, given the original nature of the position Barrow takes as his starting point, not so much the differences from the sort of programme I have already outlined but the similarities with it. There is also a considerable overlap with White's proposals. Both writers take enormous pains to deal with possible objections, and to spell out the importance of taking their own interpretations of 'communication', 'history' or whatever rather than the reader's. It is this very precision which is their undoing; for it shows up the more starkly the arbitrariness of, in White's case, the 'great choice' each pupil must make at about age 17, and in Barrow's, the duration of a given curriculum stage for two years rather than one or three or five. For different reasons, neither is likely to satisfy the first prerequisite I have suggested. For White's curriculum is to be nationally imposed rather than school-developed, and Barrow's seems quirky with regard to modern languages, and particularly science and mathematics which appear to become options at third-year level. But in both accounts we can see theorists – and philosophers at that – making practical, detailed suggestions; and that is of great merit. Barrow also examines the place of conventional school subjects with valuable clarity.

We now return to Hirst's analysis as our brief, and identify two further stages of curriculum design. We must first consider how the school's architecture, staff, traditions and external constraints will influence the way in which pupils will encounter the forms of knowledge; and we must then develop detailed schemes of work which will implement, sustain and evaluate the programme. But we must realise that there is interaction between the two levels; how children learn is a determinant of what they learn, and a decision, for example, that implementation will need a longer time-period than the traditional 35 minutes may well influence the way in which subjects are grouped or not. Neither does it follow that because mathematics and science, for instance, are separate forms of understanding, they must necessarily be separated formally between departments or faculties. What matters is that pupils are brought to see that doing mathematics and doing science involve different central concepts, different logical structures, distinctive expressions that are testable against experience, and different techniques and skills for exploring experience. On the face of it, there would seem to be some practical sense in a formal separation; but this must be weighed against the consideration that by bringing them to interact, learning and understanding may be contrived more effectively. It is a nice judgment, and we shall return to it in Chapter 7.

Let us consider, though, what sorts of decisions we can make at this stage about the general shape of the curriculum, and then look at the judgments and values involved in organising the learning. Certain matters are already clear. It is evident that we must be as careful in separating moral and religious education as with science and mathematics. In some schools, low pupil engagement with traditional RE has led to the RE lesson broadening out into areas of ME. There are dangers in this, especially when RE is all that appears on the timetable. In others, it has become fashionable (often under pressure from LEA advisers) to establish lessons in 'education for personal relationships', and 'EPR' periods are quite ubiquitous. These can become an obscure blend of RE, ME and careers education, and again seem a way of making RE more palatable rather than a fresh look at the issues raised by RE as an isolated timetable phenomenon; in short, another case of piecemeal planning, or the 'band-aid' approach to curriculum development.

I have touched in Chapter 2 on one aspect of science provision; while all must take a worthwhile course in it, leading to one 16-plus subject pass, about half the year-group are likely to want further science in years 4 and 5. Another decision must be what kind of science programme is most likely to advance a pupil's understanding of scientific thinking, bearing in mind the distinction Hirst makes between the physical and human sciences. We must remember too that these are not just decisions about science subjects; they will also impinge upon option choices for pupils deciding between the attractions for them of further science, or foreign languages, or business studies and craft skills. On the whole, an integrated science programme has a number of advantages. It cuts out superfluous areas of content, thus providing a two O-level subject certification which is none the less an excellent basis for A-level study; it offers the chance to think afresh about science for all, free from the association in many science teachers' minds of separate science O-levels with subject proficiency for its own sake; and by reducing the time requirement from that for three to two subject passes, it reduces pressure on the option columns.

A related question then arises, though, with regard to links between science and mathematics on the one hand, or science and aesthetic experience on the other. It is certainly true that much mathematics teaching would benefit from closer contact with its uses; but to go on to suggest that an explicit maths /science link is therefore essential is a step of another order. And it is difficult to see how it can easily be done when integrated science studies as a distinct area of study seem so attractive. But if a school were obliged (chiefly, perhaps, for reasons of accommodation) to split physical from biological sciences, then it would be worth looking at a physical science /maths link in perhaps the fourth and fifth years.

The link between science and the art/craft area of the curriculum has been advanced chiefly by those who advocate technology as a curriculum activity. This has been justified in two different ways. Most commonly, it is suggested that because economic success rests largely on technological skills, we must produce pupils who have been initiated into them. In Schools Council Working Paper No. 18 (1968), which led to the establishment of Project Technology, we were told that:

> Technology is an inescapable part of life and for our children this will be increasingly true in the future. More and more it will be met in home and factory, town and country, university and government. Schools therefore must foster an understanding of technology and encourage a creative attitude towards it.

This is an argument based on an instrumental view of education; because technology is 'part of life', it justifies a curriculum imperative. But road safety, pop music, even astrology can all be seen as part of life. So, for that matter, can science; but to make its everyday presence a curriculum reason for teaching it would be to distort it. Again, the reasons matter, and it is in this sense that curriculum design must be seen as a rational process. In this case, we cannot accept the proffered reason as good enough, in terms of our brief, to justify curriculum time. But it is a reason that has been advanced again of late, and the recent DES call for closer school links with industry could lead to an unintended curriculum influence. It is interesting, too, to note that a sixth-form college which has taught engineering science to A-level since 1969 has reported (*TES*, 28.1.77) that it does nothing to increase the number of potential engineers; and it was found that there was room enough within the Nuffield A-level physics syllabus for the applied-physics approach which it in essence amounted to. By the same token, a better approach in the fourth and fifth years would seem to be to initiate pupils into the basic forms of knowledge involved – scientific and mathematical thought, aesthetic consideration – which underpin the study of engineering.

The other argument offered for technology studies goes deeper. As Nuttgens (1975) puts it:

> While everybody ultimately believes that the most profound education is verbal and while the universities maintain their stranglehold on the examinations in the schools it will not be possible to escape the inevitable assumption in the schools – that practical people are stupid. . . .Why could not education start, like the Industrial Revolution, with technology?

It is by no means clear how it is proposed to do this, but the argument echoes a point made strongly by Schwab (1964) in which he discusses Aristotle's three major groups of disciplines: the theoretical, the practical and the productive. He suggests that: 'we have tended to fall into the habit of treating all disciplines proper to the schools as if they were theoretical. We manage to maintain this preoccupation in the case of the practical disciplines by ignoring them.' For our present purposes, this is a valuable reminder that pupils' curriculum experiences should be as creatively personal as we can make them, rather than a vicarious observation of a writer's, or artist's, or teacher's experience. And we shall find it useful to return to it when discussing the management of the curriculum in Chapter 5. But the discipline of the practical is not confined to practical activities, and it is difficult to see Nuttgens's argument other than as a reinforcement of the view, grounded on the Hirstian analysis, that the core curriculum should contain aesthetic experiences which can be worked out in terms of designed artefacts, where appropriate. Such a scheme will be discussed in detail in the next chapter.

So far, we can see three areas of the curriculum which may reasonably be conceived as distinct, bounded envelopes: mathematics, science and an art/craft area. The boundaries are justified partly by distinctions between the forms of knowledge, and also by plain common-sense considerations of situation and organisation. They transcend departmental distinctions between chemistry, physics and biology, and between art and craft subjects, but they do not eliminate them; neither are links between the areas excluded. Each area or faculty represents a sizeable team of staff and suggests leadership responsibilities of a more extensive nature. We are left with the task of providing experiences in what can be termed the expressive domain and the humanities. These will include history; English and drama as ways of developing thought and our own perceptions; a study of social and geographical aspects of culture; religious and moral education; and music as a fine art, which is not an explicit component of the art/craft faculty. At first sight there are many ways of proceeding. But some helpful clues are given by Hirst and Peters (1970):

> The process of developing different forms of distinct yet interrelated experience and understanding can be likened to building a jigsaw . . . the independent modes . . . must be built from the necessary interlocking elements in the curriculum. . . . If a doctrinaire insistence on integrated curriculum units may be seriously miseducative, such units nevertheless would seem to have a crucial place in really adequate curriculum planning.

It seems logical to look for patterns of interrelation which bring components together in ways which are mutually fruitful. The role of English is of particular importance, and it is difficult to justify it as a distinct faculty of its own. As Hirst and Peters observe: 'Under the label of English . . . it is now not uncommon to find concern for an understanding of other persons and of moral matters, as much as aesthetic and linguistic elements. Such subjects have become important in emphasising the connections which exist between different independent domains.' Undoubtedly, too, English skills will be constantly extended by the oral and written work that will arise in history and geography, and will benefit, too, from links with drama. Indeed, if the Bullock report's doctrine of 'language across the curriculum' means anything, it means that English should suffuse all the discourse of the curriculum, at least as an implicit presence. By making it a component of an interrelated area, we can go further and give it explicit force. And a link of this kind with history and geography would seem an obvious step to take. Such an area would form a humanities faculty, and might well include social studies and religious education. A separate faculty of the expressive arts would then link music and drama, and if English were also a component of this area, its formal influence would extend over a substantial part of the curriculum.

The expressive arts faculty would also be a convenient location for role-play based experiences in moral education. But the particular circumstances of a school and its community might favour other faculty arrangements. For example, home economics will be a personal option for pupils in years 4 and 5, but can make a contribution both to an art/craft area, and to a humanities/social studies area. It is usually found in a technical block along with art and craft, and would therefore be conveniently administered as part of a creative activities faculty. But it need not be so, and music need not be separated from such a faculty, either. It might make good sense to work out a role for music linked with art and craft, and associate home economics with a social studies faculty which could include some geography and also moral education. Then a separate humanities faculty would embrace English, history, drama and religious education. Apart from aspects of the physical layout of accommodation, such a scheme would be attractive if the school were in an area where there were sound community reasons for an emphasis on social studies. There is in any case a danger that where geography is an explicit humanities component, it will dominate to the exclusion of desirable aspects of social studies.

We can, at any rate, see that five faculties such as mathematics, science, creative activities, humanities and expressive arts will be necessary and sufficient to form a structure for a common liberal education. The place of a foreign language will be discussed in detail in Chapter 7. For the moment, it is clear our rationale cannot justify it as a compulsory element in the five-year programme. But as an instrumental curriculum component, we must give all pupils the chance of determining whether their interest and aptitude will lead them to make study of one or two foreign languages a personal choice. A languages faculty will therefore need to provide a common foreign language for all for the first two or three years, and possibly free access to a second in the third year. Pupils will then have a rational basis for their choice of further studies in the fourth and fifth year. This arrangement will require a third-year option of one or two timetabled periods, in which, say, German and Latin are set against activities which are likely to have wide appeal, and may be pursued on an interest basis without prejudice to present or future curriculum components. Thus an introductory third year second language option period would offer courses in the area of science, art and craft perhaps to those pupils who declined a wider experience of foreign languages. In this way a divisive separation of a second language set, on the basis of a questionable assessment of language ability, is avoided.

A seventh and final faculty would embrace physical activities, which are not included in the Hirstian rationale as a form of understanding, but which any normal school must plainly provide. But the basis of this provision needs examining. If we see it in instrumental terms – as offering experiences which will be of use to students as young men and women – then a regard for the current range of leisure activities will be desirable. But providing a choice between badminton, golf, horse riding and squash – to name only a few popular recreations – is often expensive. It is also true that until a pupil has found out what it is like to play, say, hockey, he cannot tell whether he likes it or not. Schools must therefore strike a balance between compulsory and voluntary activities, bearing in mind that in any event, nothing is worth doing if it cannot be done well. More emphasis should be given, too, to health education in this area of the curriculum. While aspects of this will be a part of both science and humanities, physical education ought to be more directly concerned with helping pupils to look after themselves in the sense.

Such a curriculum plan has the overarching simplicity which makes it easy to comprehend in intention, and to identify with in execution. But it is a simplicity which in no way denies complexity; for the infrastructure must be intricate and sensitive enough to give staff personal fulfilment regardless of their specialism, and motivate pupils to go beyond the minimum and strive for excellence. It must, in short, give the school its character and style so that it will foster happy and productive relations between all who work in it. The school's intentions in these areas must be clarified and made explicit, so that a set of consistent values can be both caught and taught. But in adopting a programme which aims to initiate all pupils into a liberal education, a school will be well on the way to promoting an atmosphere of optimism and fraternity.

It is a plan, too, which requires only two columns of options in years 4 and 5. For further science can be chosen from either, and combined with a foreign language from the other column; while a range of business and craft skills can be included in each. Thus personal interests can be pursued and taken to examination level, because a sound general education has been followed in the faculty structure. An option scheme will never allow every possible desire to be met; what is remarkable is that the scheme outlined allows science and languages to be continued, alongside a programme including history and creative activities, where most multiple-option schemes do not. For example, there may be a few pupils who have a flair for languages, and therefore wish to take two of them, while retaining further science. Plainly these would be able pupils, and the solution would be to arrange for either extra science, or one of the languages, to be pursued outside curriculum time. One such scheme is given in the appendix. Provided the basic curriculum structure is supportive to staff, and has been evolved as part of a deliberative process, there will be an ample fund of goodwill if an additional facility of this kind is needed to meet a pupil's special needs, or perhaps assist the school to sustain a competitive posture in a parental-choice system (Chapter 9). In any case, the only alternative solution would be to establish a third option column, and this would be a case of the tail wagging the dog. Keeping options to two columns vastly reduces timetable complication and logistic problems of accommodation and staffing, and leaves more room for the cultural richness which the common curriculum is offering to all pupils.

We can now gain a clearer view of the judgments involved in implementing this design as learning experiences. Just as our design is inspired neither by the grammar nor modern school curriculum stereotypes, but is determined by a consideration of how the common school can promote a common culture; so we shall see that in the detail of curriculum planning neither a behavioural model seeking defined outcomes, nor one based on pursuing pupils' interests, offers us what we need. Simplistic distinctions between product and process, closed and open systems and so on are of little help to teachers planning courses. Furthermore, this long-running academic argument makes it very difficult to talk about an objective in curriculum planning without being seriously misunderstood. A critique of the classical behaviourist objectives model has been offered by Stenhouse (1975) and only two general points need concern us here. First, education is not a tidy process, and although teachers certainly must have in mind the kinds of outcomes they regard as desirable, the notion that in some way the lists of objectives published in works like Bloom's *Taxonomy* (1956) are practical goals really does present a thoroughly misleading way of viewing teaching and learning. Second, the evidence of P. Taylor (1970) shows that when teachers plan courses, their approach is very different:

> To some extent, the way in which teachers think about curriculum planning is an inversion of how the theorists think about it. For the theorist, curriculum planning usually starts by stating aims and objectives . . . followed by a description of the learning experiences necessary. . . . Teachers, on the other hand, appear to start, understandably enough, with the context of teaching, follow this with a consideration of the kind of learning situation likely to interest and involve their pupils and only after this consider the purposes which their teaching is to serve.

If this is true, it shows again how the study of education has stressed the theoretic rather than the practical arts. It shows also how a planning model which, in opposition to that based on behavioural objectives, stresses the teaching process as rather a successsion of responses to the pupils' changing needs and interests, can easily lead a teacher away from an agreed general strategy. Wilson (1971) has, however, made a helpful philosophical study of the concept of 'interest' which shows how valuable it can be when the teacher uses it with care.

The process model is more attractive, and Stenhouse gives a useful account of it. He notes the shortcomings of the behaviourist means-end model, and looks beyond the process model 'towards the specification of principles of procedure which refer to teacher activity'. It is an approach which takes into account an important distinction made by Eisner (1969), whose instructional objectives are essentially behavioural, and 'will develop forms of behaviour whose characteristics are known beforehand'. Against these Eisner sets another kind of objective:

> Expressive objectives differ considerably from instructional objectives. An expressive objective does not specify the behaviour the student is to acquire after having engaged in one or more learning activities. An expressive objective describes an educational encounter: it identifies a situation in which children are to work, a problem with which they are to cope, a task in which they are to engage; but it does not specify what from that encounter, situation, problem or task they are to learn. . . . An expressive objective is evocative rather than prescriptive.

If we have in mind both these kinds of objectives in Eisner's sense, we can use the term with confidence and, partly if not wholly with Stenhouse, '. . . set about curriculum design by attempting to define the classroom process in terms of what the teacher is to do at the level of principles and what the content is. In such a case our statement about a curriculum would be an answer to the question: how is the teacher to handle what?' And if we go back to the teacher as planner in Taylor's description, we see that the central task of curriculum management in the school is to make the curriculum design at once so accessible and so portable that the teacher associates it indivisibly with 'the context of teaching'. In other words, if a second-year humanities team is meeting to consider the design of a unit on the Greek city state, teachers will think of the context as the response of pupils to the ideas which they see as essential if a common understanding of the concept is to be achieved. In this way the purpose can become the starting point, and to think of specific pupils can be particularly helpful, since the work will need to meet the response of the whole ability range. Possibly the team might agree to prepare a background sheet to support a direct input by each group's teacher, followed perhaps by the writing or recording of playlets to illustrate key concepts but in smaller groups. Then all could be brought together for exchanged performance and criticism, with follow-up learning packs at different ability levels to complete the initial phase of the work. In the discussion, the teacher's objectives will be expressive; but in framing the support materials instructional objectives will be paramount. And the choice of content will reflect – as will the method – the underlying brief to select from a definition of the culture.

A useful planning device is Bloom's concept of mastery learning (1971). The discussion of this in Lawton (1975) is particularly helpful:

> Bloom does not dispute that pupils have different aptitudes for various subjects but we have to ask whether low aptitude simply excuses a teacher for failure to teach. . . . The most important message from Bloom, however, is that schools must have a variety of instructional devices available.

It must be recognised, too, that there is a danger that the concept of mastery may imply that at some point we get to the end of what is to be taught; and Bloom considers that the concept is most appropriate when the subject matter implies a closed model of instruction. But as Lawton says, there is no reason why mastery learning should not find application in a flexibly planned curriculum.

It has been necessary in this chapter to survey the less bewitching ground that lies between the high peaks of curriculum design, and the foothills of faculty organisation which will be explored in the next chapter. It is an uncomfortable halfway stage between the general and the particular, because the precise form the overarching notion of the common culture curriculum will take in terms of faculty structure will be a function of the individual school. But certainly the successful implementation of a curriculum design affecting the deep structure of a school depends on its expression in terms which make sense to all the interested groups associated with it, and which can be readily understood both as a broad educational aim and as a set of pupil experiences.

Chapter 4

Faculties and the Organisation of Learning

The pupil's view of his timetable is still, in most comprehensive schools, of a collection of subjects occupying eight 35-minute periods, five days a week. This will be most marked in the fourth and fifth years, because of subject-based multiple-option schemes; but even in the first year or two, groupings of subjects under headings like Inquiry, Humanities or Social Studies are unusual. Where attempted, they run sometimes for only the first year, and rarely continue until the third. And a study by Adams (1976) suggests that with humanities schemes in particular, the lack of coherent curriculum planning raises substantial doubts about the value of many of them.

Yet it is clear already that a common culture curriculum must proceed on the basis of forms of understanding, or on a concept of disciplines, rather than on subjects; and that the advantages of interrelation lead to a structure which, within six or seven faculties, can meet our brief to provide both a liberal education and coverage of key instrumental areas. We have also reviewed the kinds of judgments which must be made in taking such a programme to the point where separate faculties and a small option provision can be defined generally in terms of existing subjects. Now we must see whether such a faculty structure for a school can be organised on the ground, and in particular what new strategies for organisation and pedagogy are likely to be needed. So far, we can adduce sound educational reasons for suggesting that a curriculum organised on these lines is more appropriate for the comprehensive school than what is currently on offer. We need to see how practical it can be; what sort of demands it will make; and how they compare with the demands made of staff and pupils in the subject and option centred curriculum.

The Learning Milieu

Pupils see school as a whole, and so must we. The first task is therefore to consider whether a faculty structure, as a way of implementing a common curriculum, implies any general characteristics of organisation which will be more or less common to all faculties. Our aim is to initiate pupils of all abilities into a programme which will give each of them a general education. We must try to ensure not only that each pupil achieves mastery of the key concepts and areas of knowledge, but also that each pupil is encouraged to extend his understanding to the limit of his capacity. On the one hand, pupils with learning difficulties must be led to overcome them, while always enjoying the same access as other pupils to the richness of the curriculum; on the other, able pupils must be stimulated to go further and venture more widely. And in between, we have pupils who will extend their horizons if the school climate encourages them to seize opportunities and of itself imposes no limits to the way they view their own potential. As Bloom has observed, there is nothing sacrosanct about the normal distribution; it describes random processes rather than intentional ones. If we cannot be optimistic about pupil achievement, and are content to confine it within the bounds of examination statistics or the pupil's response in the environment of a previous school, we are surely in breach of what should be our dominant professional attitude as teachers; as heirs to a noble tradition of initiating newcomers to our world and its culture.

We need a climate, and a style of doing things and judging people, which will promote these ends. The climate must be both secure and flexible. Staff and pupils must know where they stand; nothing undermines the confidence of a teacher or the response of a pupil more certainly than a feeling of mutual confusion about the nature of the discourse between them. But the style of their relationship must be open enough to stimulate enterprise. Two things follow. First, a variety of learning strategies will be needed; and second, there must be a resource facility to support these strategies. The implication of both is that the basic period must be long enough to give the teacher room to manoeuvre. He will need to set up and check a pattern of group and individual work, and pupils will need time to organise source materials. A minimum unit would be about 50 minutes, and there would be 5 or 6 of these in the day. The advantage of a 70-minute period is that two fall conveniently into the morning and into the afternoon session, and many teachers in any case like a double 35-minute period.

We may draw two further conclusions. The first concerns the grouping of staff. If a variety of approaches is needed, much will be gained by encouraging staff to work together in teams in planning the course. And this may well go further, to the point where advantage is taken of a group of staff and their individual skills in organising the teaching. The fact that in several faculties subjects are being interrelated at once reinforces a team approach. This will therefore be an important aspect of the work of a head of faculty.

The other conclusion concerns the grouping of pupils. If the aim is to make it possible for staff and pupils to respond to the opportunities for learning created by the curriculum, then staff will need easy access to materials across the whole ability range; and pupils will need to feel that they are unshackled and unlabelled, and free to take advantage and set their sights higher without the disturbance of a move from one ability set to another. The indication that a non-streamed format is called for is inescapable, and I have argued elsewhere (1976) that such an organisation must be a key aspect of the common curriculum in action.

Non-streaming

I have touched on this issue in Chapter 2, and shall return to pupil grouping in Chapter 9 in the wider context of the school. The need here is to consider the non-streamed format as a vital aid to curriculum implementation. It is important to stress that if non-streaming is seen as an arrangement where pupils of widely differing abilities are seated side by side and doing the same thing, it is as perverse and indefensible as the streamed system, where the assumption is made that a class of pupils has the same ability and can therefore work from the same textbook and the same blackboard for lesson after lesson. What it does mean is that the teacher has all his options open; he can regard the class as a unit if this best serves his objectives, or organise it into a variety of groups, or individualise the work. Quite often, pupils' own friendship groups will be a sound basis; but if it makes sense, there is no reason why a group of pupils with, say, a talent for algebra should not work together as an informal ability set. For the set will almost certainly be constituted differently next week, when the topic is topology and their responses and aptitudes are different.

It is worth recognising, too, that there are positive advantages in arranging for some kinds of learning to be on a complete mixed-ability basis. For example, discussion in humanities work often shows (given a sensitive, aware teacher) that a pupil lacking the ability to shine on paper has a far shrewder understanding of the issues, and can make more original suggestions, than the naturally convergent child who finds his way effortlessly into top sets. It is worth noting that there is some support for this in a finding of the Cognitive Research Trust that some very interesting solutions to cognitive problems have been produced by children whose IQs are quite low. De Bono (1976) insists that there is not necessarily a correlation between high IQ and skill in thinking.

The basic pattern of organisation is now taking shape. And if we are to take full advantage of staffing, the unit for grouping pupils will be as small as we can make it. Usually a group of 25 to 30 is possible, with adjustment to meet special needs. If mixed-ability forms of this size are chosen as the pastoral unit, then the same forms will do as teaching groups. The additional advantage of a team-taught faculty will be, though, that a number of groups can be timetabled together and thus allow a range of group sizes to fit different strategies. The blocking of these groups will depend on the size of the school. Three or four forms of entry give a population in each year of 90 or 120, and this is a convenient minimum size block, allowing a team of 3 or 4 staff to be mounted. Thus for a school in the common 6 to 8 f.e. range, this block would correspond to half a year group. In a 5-form entry school, it might be convenient to take a half-year of 75, in three groups of 25, and if necessary keep these groups as a separate construction from 5 pastoral forms. In some faculties, though, the whole year group may be a better unit. For example, humanities will need teachers representing a variety of specialisms; certainly English, history and geography in most cases, perhaps with religious education, social studies, science, art and classics as well at various stages in the 5-year course. If a whole-year group of 180 pupils are blocked out together, a team of 6 or 7 staff can be formed which will provide a valuable diverse resource. The same will hold good in creative activities, where the whole range of art, craft and housecraft activities will be represented. Furthermore, teaching groups in this faculty will need to be nearer 20 in size if current trends in these subjects are to be maintained. This can obviously be done very conveniently across the whole-year group, leading to a team of perhaps 8 or 9 staff depending in this case, again, on which year it is in the entire 5-year programme.

We can see similar advantages in the structure for games and recreational activities, where variety of staff expertise is at a premium. But in science, a half-year group of 90 to three teachers will give an adequate spread between the three contributory subjects of physics, chemistry and biology, and make the provision of apparatus much less costly than if twice this number were to be taught at once. Space is another limitation. In the nature of things, the interrelated areas like humanities and creative activities will include two or three or more subjects, along with the areas of the school normally allocated to them; while languages and mathematics as single subjects will lay claim to fewer classrooms and, therefore, will best be taught as half-year groups.

At the extremes

We are almost ready to look at faculty organisation in detail. But we must return first to the nature of the provision for the two extreme groups of pupils about whom concern is often expressed: the remedial and the gifted. It is clear that a curriculum based on a view of our culture must offer great scope to the gifted child. It may be argued that such a child's gifts may lie exclusively in mathematics, or music, and that he should be allowed to concentrate on them; that a particular rather than a general education is better. But for every prodigy who supported that view, one could find another who did not. Our task must be to see that the school has the intellectual resources to extend such pupils, and a flexible enough structure to make it possible for staff to extend that resource. Surprising views are expressed on how flexible it should be: for example, a headmaster of Charterhouse recently told a conference that 'gifted boys have suffered from the stringent demands of examinations which have changed the whole attitude to work in our schools'. Yet those who so readily espouse public examinations are often those who stress intellectual standards. It seems sensible to conclude that because a common curriculum, in an unstreamed format, obliges us to extend all our pupils, we can safeguard the gifted child by arranging for staff to devise materials and strategies which will be readily available. Shrewd leadership by heads of faculties will be essential.

The needs of remedial pupils may be met in some schools by hiving them off into a separate department. This is essentially a divisive approach, and pupils tend to respond by living down to the expectations the school evidently has of them. A further objection is that it lumps together pupils whose difficulties may be of many different kinds. Indeed, it seems helpful to move away from the limiting concept of remedial education; it means either a small number with severe difficulties, usually in reading, or a very large number of pupils in the sense that all of us have an inadequate skill in some area or other which needs remedying. If we talk instead of the needs of slow learners, it places these problems where they belong, in the mainstream of curriculum organisation; and helps us to make a provision which recognises individual difficulties in subjects other than English. And just as these pupils are part of the same curriculum, so also should be their teachers. There is no reason why staff who teach slow learners should not belong to faculty teams for at least part of their commitment, and thus gain an insight into the school's aims for all pupils and know that they share the same status as all staff.

The main effort to improve slow learners will therefore be a part of ordinary faculty organisation. If there is a member of staff whose responsibility is to coordinate this work, then it helps if a teacher in each faculty is asked to liaise with him and promote the faculty's response to these needs. This would involve looking closely at the range of materials to check that the language used, and visual treatment, are sufficiently varied, and special study guides produced as necessary. It also means working closely with the head of faculty in discussions of teaching strategies with staff; there is an in-service education function here and in a school with a severe slow-learner problem, these liaison appointments would be just as important as that of the coordinator, who will also have a training function for all staff and will arrange for induction courses on equipment and approaches for new staff while keeping everyone up to the mark on new equipment, tests and strategies by importing specialists or arranging lectures.

All staff can be involved in the faculty operation so far. But there are two further ways in which remedial help must be given for a number of pupils, if the right diagnosis and treatment are to be offered. On the one hand, a specialist teacher can be made a supernumerary member of a team, looking closely at the work of remedial pupils and giving them extra help to understand basic concepts; and on the other, it will be necessary for some pupils to be withdrawn from faculties so that specific help using specialist equipment can be provided. An advantage of faculty organisation is that extra 'floating' team members can so readily be worked into the system. As for withdrawal, the important thing seems to be to move quickly to identify difficulties when pupils transfer from junior school, and capitalise on the fresh horizons so many pupils glimpse in the new school by mounting a vigorous campaign in the first year. This may mean withdrawal for, say, extra English help from science as well as humanities periods; for staffing cuts have bitten deep into the part-time provision which is so useful here, and flexible timetabling on demand is not easy. But all staff will accept this if it means that by the second year reading ages of 6½ to 8 can be lifted to 9 or 10 in many cases. The inconvenience of reorienting withdrawn pupils when they return to a practical lesson is nothing compared with the disaffection of the child for whom too little has been done, too late.

The key subjects here will be English and mathematics. After pupils have settled in on transfer, general testing is advisable since junior school estimates can be unreliable. In English, a test that checks comprehension is essential, to ensure that the child's reading is not just a matter of 'barking at print'. In maths, individual maths profiles are vital since only one concept may be weak. No single satisfactory test exists and teachers' assessments are therefore important. For withdrawals, a pupil may need between 2 and 4 sessions weekly of about 35 minutes, usually with 4 or 5 pupils in a group although 10 is possible, and individual help in some cases. Social reasons are important in the group formation, and single-sex groups sometimes work better. Sixth-form pupils can be very helpful as aides to teachers in a group.

Within faculties, the response of staff can be very variable. Tape can be a powerful medium, even when used as straight reading by staff from books. Picture cards are useful and can be home-made easily by gutting the cheaper books; they stimulate discussion, writing or role play. Some staff sense instinctively that pictures can work better than words, while others will need to be shown how to vary their approach. The good remedial teacher will help staff identify a child's difficulty by checking on his confidence, phonic grasp and motivation, and aim to create a bond of complete trust. New staff will need to be shown the special facilities of the room set aside for special help with English, and another room for maths help is most desirable. Quite small spaces created by partitions if necessary will do at a pinch; but lockable filing cabinets and shelves for apparatus will be essential. A useful spin-off from involving new staff in helping pupils with learning difficulties within faculties is that often a teacher will gain a new insight to carry over into his general teaching.

In a comprehensive school with a representative spread of ability, and where there are no social reasons for expecting learning difficulties to be other than average, it seems likely that in the first year between 12 and 15 per cent will be getting some kind of help in the ways described. By the fifth year the proportion will have dropped to 3 per cent at the most, and these will be pupils who often value the social contact with their specialist teacher for English or reading help. If faculty provision is well organised, then no more than 5 per cent of the total staffing allocation need be set aside expressly for specialist remedial teaching.

Resources

The needs of slow learners serve as an introduction to the school's wider provision of resources for learning. This fashionable phrase of the late 1960s led to talk of resource-based learning, with the implication of individualised learning systems and, in some new schools, the construction of a central resource facility as the focus of curriculum activity. As so often happens in the volatile climate of educational innovation, the part is taken for the whole, and quite soon those who are not swept along by the new nostrum are presumed to be against it. The argument becomes polarised, and a rational appreciation suddenly becomes very difficult – particularly to the progressive teacher who can become confused by the political fervour with which the new idea is embraced by advisers, or at conferences. It is a heresy to take an aspect of a complex issue and represent it as the millennial essence, and it does much harm to the cause of enlightenment in education. In this case it is very clear that an innovating school will need more than textbooks and wallcharts if it is to enable its staff to bring all the pupils inside an ambitious programme of knowledge, skills and attitudes. Without doubt, books will still be the most useful of its aids to learning; a great variety of them rather than a few sets of standard texts. Indeed, to some extent the school library will need to be taken out of its confines and brought into the faculty areas – although a library facility for reference and recreation will always be required. In this respect, figures for the optimal number of library books per pupil can be misleading; if the books are in use, the library shelves may look bare. The concept of book resources must take into account both the school's active and passive needs.

Staff will need to make up worksheets of a high standard where they are necessary as a steering mechanism between different modes of teaching or types of resource. For high quality, cheap reprographics, an offset-litho machine is unequalled and should be a higher PTA priority than the overrated minibus. Ancillary staffing provision will include a staff secretary as copy typist for manuscripts; another part-timer to operate the litho machine; and ideally another for artwork and graphics, using a variety of type faces (a jumbo typewriter is invaluable for materials for slow learners) to enliven the product. A reprographic centre of this kind could be used conveniently for storing inter-faculty audio-visual aids like 16mm projectors and TV equipment, as well as a supply point to all faculties for basic stationery requirements. Such a step helps budgetary control, too.

Other aids will be filmstrips, slide viewers and tape recorders along with learning packs or collections of *realia*. The question of how these materials are to be classified, stored and retrieved comes back to the school's curriculum aims. If resource or inquiry based learning is being advocated for its own sake, a central resource facility, with optical indexing and additional ancillary help on a considerable scale, will be justified. But this would seem an unwise rationale for any school. The central experiences are to do with forms of knowledge and understanding rather than styles of learning, which come second and not first. Otherwise it would be like deciding where to go for a holiday on the basis of whatever clothes are left in the suitcase. But this is not to deny for a moment the intimate connexion between form, content and method; it is only to point out that after the curriculum brief is fixed, then decisions can be taken as to how to organise the resources. I suspect that in practice, elaborate indexing systems are rarely used to their full potential; most resources are linked with particular faculties, and inter-faculty usage really requires only a straightforward cross-referenced subject and topic catalogue, which has the advantage of easy circulation and access. This is a further reason for avoiding inter-related areas which draw on more than one faculty, like the 'Enquiry' scheme described in the previous chapter. Clear thinking about curriculum design keeps systems simple; and only reasonably simple systems allow new staff to absorb the school learning styles quickly and adapt them to their own talents. Complexity makes for rigidity, and usually costs more anyway.

It is therefore perfectly possible to adapt a school to a faculty based common curriculum without presupposing a large resource centre. A resource facility in each faculty will do the trick, and may amount to a few enlarged cupboards, a full set of four-drawer filing cabinets and some tray storage.

As to the layout of the space, it is best to consider this on a faculty basis.

Humanities

Clarity about curriculum concepts here is essential. The ease with which interrelation can become integration in teachers' minds is pinpointed by Shipman (1974):

> This can be seen most clearly in the schools' response to early documents from the (Keele humanities) project stressing that integration did not mean fitting together bits from different subjects but rather meant utilizing the unique contribution of those individual subjects. Few schools seemed to grasp this idea or even consider it. Even after two years of trial most were proud of their success in breaking down the barriers between subjects. Consequently team teaching . . . was usually seen, not as a way of using specialists, but as a way of producing general teachers.

Given our curriculum brief, we must see humanities as a faculty which leads children to look at man and his development not by the construction of dubious supra-concepts, but by reclassifying knowledge in terms of the contributory disciplines. We thus pose an area of inquiry, such as: how does man develop civilisation? And the head of faculty can then work out strategies with the heads of English, history, geography and religious education. Each of these will want to ensure that his own subject's objectives are met. In geography, for example, concepts of location, distribution and exchange; in history perhaps of judgment, values and knowledge domains. And when the resulting strategies are discussed with, say, the team of first-year teachers who are to introduce them and develop the teaching approach, a further reclassification and objectifying process will take place. They will take as their starting point: what kinds of activities and outcomes do I seek in the context of my own particular discipline? How should the work of pupils be chosen and organised so that they are led to ask the right questions about my discipline? For humanities, on this thesis of integration, is not simply a field of study based on man. It is based rather on certain specific kinds of question concerning man's development bearing directly on the disciplines concerned. A central task for the head of humanities will be the resolution of lines of control which are horizontal in terms of year groups, but vertical in terms of the subjects. The outline of such a scheme might be:

Year 1: Introductory section based on reminiscences.
Communication; basic reference techniques.
Man and nature: origins of the universe and earth's structure; of life, and creation myths; origins of man.
Man's needs: food, spiritual, shelter, communication, kinship and society.
Man the citizen: a section on the middle ages.
A concluding section on local studies (more conveniently taken at the warmer end of the school year).

Year 2: The concept of evidence: language; archaeology and documents; physical features and maps.
The Mediterranean civilization: art; architecture; literature; religion; politics; mining and primitive technology.
An extra-European civilization: perhaps Imperial China, or perhaps America as a multi-racial society.
Discovery and the Renaissance.

Year 3: Poverty and the family: In England now; in sixteenth-century England; in India now.
Wider horizons: underdevelopment and aid in the world.
Voyages of discovery: Europe around AD 1500; motives for voyages; famous explorations; the conquest of Peru and Mexico.
A subject interlude: poetry; historical exercise; glaciation.
Limits to growth: economic; social; political and moral problems.

Years 4 and 5: The five-year course may now lead to O-level and CSE examinations in English, history and geography. For the scheme at Sheredes School, on which this programme is based, it was necessary, given the range of mode 1 examinations available in 1969, to plan these as mode 3 exams. Half the total marks in each subject are allocated to course work, distinguishing, in history and geography, understanding; organisation; initiative; application; participation and breadth of study. In English, written course work is assessed for variety and quality; vocabulary and appropriateness of language; breadth and sensitivity of reading; originality; group project contribution and presentation. One-tenth of the marks are allocated to oral work, individually assessed. It is likely that a similar scheme could now be developed using recently available mode 1 examinations. Remaining marks go as usual to a formal end-of-course examination.

In organising the work over these two years, common themes are studied in each subject:

ENGLISH: Communication, childhood, industry and urbanisation, life in towns and cities, war, Africa.

HISTORY: Industrial revolution, transport changes, urbanisation, twentieth-century world with particular reference to Britain at war, Africa, Europe 1919-39, Russia, China.

GEOGRAPHY: Industry, urbanisation, communications, Africa; and local studies are incorporated into these three themes.

(English is a single subject, embracing both language and literature. The distinction seems pointless, other than as a way of churning out an extra examination pass.)

Classroom organisation proceeds in two ways, or combinations of them. Either each teacher uses or adapts common materials developed by the whole year team, retaining his group of pupils; or the group rotates between teachers offering their specialism. In general, the second pattern becomes more dominant as a pupil moves from year 1 to year 3, and prevails in the fourth and fifth years. Thus in the first year the first pattern may prevail, giving the advantage of greater stability between teacher and pupil at a time of transition. In the second year a 4-week rotation pattern may be convenient. In the third, a similar arrangement may give greater emphasis to the separate disciplines. The faculty structure gives scope for tailormade variation. For instance, fourth-year groups may rotate weekly between English, history and geography, while in the fifth year even tighter continuity can be assured by having virtually a 6-day timetable, with two consecutive lessons in each subject.

Before leaving this key faculty, two final points should be

made. First, there is adequate scope for making religious education an intimate part of the approach. The emphasis will be on exposing religious interpretations of life; bringing pupils to see what it means to adhere to a religion; and presenting elements in our own culture which reflect religious values and concepts. In the first year, topics might include: the siege of Masada; signs and symbols; sun worship. In the second, the birth of Christianity; festivals and sacred places. In the third, sacred writings; Jesus; works like *Lord of the Flies*. While in the fourth and fifth years, topics will include man and fear; the world council of churches; Hinduism; anti-semitism; the Jew and the Arab.

Second, it must be stressed that a completely non-streamed organisation can be preserved for all five years. The mode 3 CSE and O-level examinations can be dovetailed together so as to give all the advantages of a common system of examination. Indeed, it will be seen that a common culture curriculum can be established wholly in terms of the existing system, even though in some areas the divided exam structure leads inevitably to separate O-level and CSE groups by the fourth or fifth year. But by this time pupils well understand that they are valued for their own individual sakes, and virtually select themselves into these two broad groups. In humanities, it means that a pupil can be given a choice of ways of looking at the topic of, say, urbanisation; choice is not extrinsic between subjects, but intrinsic within faculties. And with staff guidance and his own self-knowledge, he can choose a way which matches his interest and ability, yet maps exactly onto the brief for the whole curriculum.

Creative Activities

It has been necessary to look at humanities in some detail as an example of an interrelated area in which vital issues of balance and continuity, content and method, aims and organisation are revealed. Another popular area for interrelation is one that links art and craft, but it is unusual to find this worked out as a five-year scheme. I have written elsewhere (1974) of the general aims such a programme might have. In summary, we are concerned both with the acquisition of skills in the contributory subjects, and with a creative response centred on a genuine integration of disciplines in terms of design problems. It is interesting to note in passing that words like 'community', 'social' and 'design' have become debased currency in education, to use at one's peril; like an aerosol, they can be sprayed onto a phrase to give an instant gloss of excitement and novelty. It is rare now to find an LEA adviser-for art; the magic words 'and design' have usually been added. But it is by no means clear what they mean. However, it makes sense for a creative activities faculty to concentrate in the first two or three years of a five-year course on an approach which uses, like humanities, a weak theory of integration and develops skills through mainly instructional objectives; moving in the fourth and fifth years to a problem-centred approach developing skills through stronger integration and expressive objectives.

Let us suppose a team of 9 staff in the first year of a six-form entry of 180 pupils. Their separate areas might be: home economics; wood; metal; dress; pottery; painting; graphics; printing; fabric and collage. Instead of straight rotation, it is better to use staff in sub-teams with a 5-week rotation module. Then each teacher can take the same group twice over the year, giving greater continuity and contact time. There might be some thematic unity, like 'light and shade', but the specialist needs of each discipline take priority. Although home economics is best organised as a part of this faculty if it is part of the same building, it is best regarded as an instrumental rather than liberal element of the curriculum and attempts to bring it within a theme need great circumspection. In a first-year programme like this, where the materials are less resistant the aims can go beyond craft skills to more creative modes.

In the second year the same pattern continues. In the third, the rotation of modules can be varied to give a 10-week continuous run in all but home economics and painting, to suit staff needs. The groupings might be: art and pottery; wood and metalwork; fabric and dress. The longer sessions allow greater depth and facilitate a greater degree of integration.

The fourth year sees a distinct shift. Staff are allocated to three groupings: human aids and extensions; living and working space; and communications. These are concerned respectively with ergonomics and craft skills; problems of direct experience (new designs, modelmaking); and problems related to forms of expression in visual communication using signs and symbols (art work; a critical approach to advertising). Each group team appoints its leader, and develops a bank of project ideas from which, in each of the three groups, a pupil selects two projects. The year thus sees the completion of six projects, which might look at town planning and caravan design under living and working space; and designing cutlery and an office desk under human aids and extensions. A design brief is produced for each project, and 45 per cent of the marks in the concluding CSE mode 3 examination in Design will go to the pupil's coursework, as a recorded design process and as a final product, over this year. The aim of the faculty head will be to promote a sensitive and intuitive staffing structure. Pupil groups form in a fluid way around staff as the projects develop and may move off into separate rooms. As in humanities, there are real disadvantages in too open an arrangement of space. Open-plan layouts make the control of materials more difficult and amplify noise. A cellular structure, used flexibly with open doors and close staff team-work gives the advantage of separation when needed which can be of great advantage to teacher and pupil alike. Neither open-plan nor separate classrooms is right; the architect must exploit the space so as to reflect the distinct but integrated use the faculty will make of it.

Experience shows that a curriculum area on these lines can lead to marked pupil involvement and self-motivation, with much extra work being done at home, perhaps to the point where it must be curbed lest other faculties suffer. In the fifth year, pupils have a choice of two problems over the year; one based on a specific craft, the other on a project. Topics might be: stage design; fabric screen printing; clay sculpture; silversmithing; from thread to garment. The balance of CSE examination marks goes on the final project and diary. In this way, each student is led to find autonomy in making his own aesthetic judgments, based on a broad general education in subject structures which reflect art as a form of life. While the aims of a liberal education are met, there is a close mesh with the real world and the problems that must be faced in home and industry. It is difficult to see why, on a commonsense view, any student should be denied such a programme; but without a planned five-year rationale it is difficult to see how even one student could be offered it.

If it were felt necessary, the end-of-course examination could include a written paper carrying perhaps 20 per cent of the marks. This could be based on a study of design developments, and might include questions on the Art Nouveau movement; surrealism; Brunel; or high-rise dwellings. Such an element might be appropriate to a parallel O-level examination. It is worth adding that suitable mode 1 O-level examinations in design studies of the sort discussed here are now available.

Science

We now turn to a five-year programme which will lead for all pupils to at least a single certification in integrated science, and for those choosing to take extra science as an option in years 4 and 5, a double certification at either O-level or CSE. In the first two years, a programme based on Nuffield Combined Science is attractive, with perhaps a shift of approach to give less of a programmed course and less factual recall, and more emphasis on developing skills and an insight into scientific method. There can be a move away from content towards topics as a way of generating a variety of responses across the ability range. The approach is based on mastery learning, leaning heavily on the teacher's understanding of individual pupils to vary the learning structure. If three teachers are timetabled with a half-year of 90 pupils, therefore, the same teacher will remain with his non-streamed group for the whole year. There is evidence that pupils' attitudes to science are much influenced by their experience of it in these early years. The wise head of science will therefore keep a close eye on these staff teams, and might well be a member of one of them. Regular tests at the end of each section are a useful check on progress.

In the third year a greater emphasis on content reflects the effective start of a three-year examination course. The Schools Council Integrated Science Project materials (SCISP, published as *Patterns*) are a satisfactory course basis for the whole ability range. Careful choice of topics allows concrete concepts to be stressed, and in any case the SCISP course has strong links with the humanities area of the curriculum which makes it very suitable for a common curriculum programme. Biological concepts like photosynthesis, digestion, respiration and the circulation of the blood can be used very effectively, with a continued emphasis on individual structuring.

In the fourth year it is likely that at least half the year group will opt for extra science, and at Sheredes boys and girls opt in almost equal numbers. Those not opting continue the integrated course begun in the third year, leading to a mode 3 CSE in integrated science. (It is an interesting comment on the reactionary attitudes which teacher control appears to have preserved in CSE boards, that the official title of this truly integrated examination must be general science. Similarly, our experience in humanities with parallel mode 3 exams in CSE and O-level in three subjects has shown a much more sensitive response, ironically, from the O-level board concerned than from the teacher-dominated CSE board.) However, recently a mode 1 CSE course in integrated science has become available in many areas.

A degree of staff rotation in half-year teams can be introduced in the third year, so that specialist skills can be utilised. This pattern is extended further in the fourth year. Pupils opting for extra science need not at this stage be identified as SCISP (a course leading to two O-levels in integrated science) or double CSE candidates. For the latter, certification may be offered ultimately in human biology and in physical science; or if preferred in a mode 3 double-subject CSE in integrated science. A mode 1 examination of the latter type will shortly be available.

In science periods in core time, as opposed to the extra science option periods, 4 staff are needed so as to allow two parallel sets for double-subject students (taking extra science in either option) and two parallel sets for students taking just the core science leading to a single subject CSE. In the fifth year, general arrangements are the same but the two parallel double-subject sets are split into one for SCISP, and one for two CSE entries. Although SCISP is very much a demanding O-level course, it is possible to enter up to 30 per cent of the year group for it with pleasing results. The whole five-year integrated course is as attractive to staff as to pupils, and there is no difficulty in recruiting scientists with specialist subject qualifications to teach it. Furthermore, the fact that the staff must regard themselves as members all of the same team can make for a very productive and harmonious association.

Mathematics

If the curriculum aim is to initiate pupils into mathematics as a form of understanding, the case for a course which is based on a modern mathematics approach is really irresistible. But great care is needed in making sure the immense mathematical benefits of this approach penetrate to all pupils, and not just those with mathematical gifts. This calls for a close-knit faculty organisation and especial refinement in assessing the learning of individual pupils. There is no doubt that as a subject, it is much less accessible, in the sense of promoting a ready engagement, than those in the humanities curriculum area. In both cases pupils will be encouraged to seek abstractions, but the symbolic expressions of mathematics are at once more sudden and less human; they are not connected up to people. The style of maths learning must therefore be more closely controlled, less open-textured than in humanities; the young probationary teacher, mesmerised by brilliant demonstration lessons in his training course in which a whole class is led to mathematise (as the jargon goes) from nothing more than perhaps a handful of numbers as the blackboard starter, will soon discover that dogged patience, unremitting attention to detail and lots of talk about individual pupils is worth a great deal more than flashy inspiration. But at least mathematics staff can call upon an extensive range of published text and cards, while their colleagues in humanities must match the greater openness of their transactions with supple material fashioned from their own resources.

In the first two years, the recently available SMP workcards form a useful basic course. After each section a short diagnostic test is available, and pupils can follow a number of alternative paths on an individual basis. There seems little justification for elaborate computer-based learning systems here; but there is a good case for them in the top year of junior schools, where they would be invaluable at identifying and correcting individual weaknesses. In the secondary school, these skills are available from specialist teachers; in the junior school a child has about an even chance that his teacher has passed mathematics O-level.

Abler pupils can pass quickly through the card system and move on either to higher level worksheets, or to texts like SMP Book 1. Investigations and games will also be used. Below-average pupils will have their weaknesses spotted, and can be cycled onto remedial materials along with the help of specialist teachers in the team. It is important, though, that work on cards is not the only kind of mathematical activity; indeed, work in groups or on a class basis will be essential if pupils are to be exposed to the cut and thrust of ideas. Individualised learning systems, like the ILEA's SMILE project, are open to this objection. An exclusive diet of worksheets may make control problems easier, but it denies pupils the chance to expose mathematical concepts to dispute and discussion.

By the third year most pupils will leave the cards for SMP books E and F, with the same access to higher and lower level work. To ensure continuity during this period of basic learning, there will be a ring binder in the department for each pupil, containing assessment cards from his point of entering the school and giving test results and assessments from each teacher for each unit of the course. Without such a system, there is a danger that a pupil may get to the end of the third year without really understanding, say, binary arithmetic. In addition, teachers will keep separate records in a record book of performance on homework and classwork. The third-year work will be more formalised, with a greater use of published texts.

In the first term of the fourth year a preliminary distribution of pupils between, say, 2 O-level and 6 CSE groups (for an 8-form entry) can be made and refined by testing and discussion among staff and students and at parents' evenings. By the summer term, these sets can still sustain one or two changes but few are likely. There will be about 10 per cent of the year group who would be ungraded in the CSE; it will be remembered that this examination is not intended to reach down to the bottom 20 per cent of the ability range in a given subject but the motivating effect of the common curriculum makes some stretching possible – particularly in humanities for the reasons already given. These non-examination candidates will emerge during the fourth year and will need in the fifth to be placed in perhaps two groups of up to 10 each, which need not be isolated as such but will respond to such special attention as staffing will allow. A special course may be devised for them, perhaps based on SMP books E and F in the fourth year and moving to tailormade materials in the fifth. In some areas a local certificate of mathematical competence has been developed for such pupils and this can be helpful. Abler pupils, on the other hand, will follow a course based on SMP books X, Y and Z, with the usual supplementary worksheets and problem-oriented material.

The course outlined is but one way in which such a programme might be developed. But it is one which can bring worthwhile mathematical experience within reach of almost all the year group. It is interesting that the significantly titled Schools Council 'Maths for the Majority' materials will be used only by the 10 per cent in the non-examination groups. The mode of team teaching which seems most effective is one which in general keeps teacher and class together for each year, but involves all staff in planning and the development of assessment and teaching materials both as a department and as year teams. Frequent and regular meetings are essential and will of course take place, in general, out of school time. As for layout, a scheme which permits the three groups in each half-year to be separate enough to give coherence, yet allows easy exchange between them and a feeling of permeability, will be very effective. This means a carpeted area with some rigid and some moveable partitions, and books and materials easily available from trolleys and shelves in teaching areas as well as a local resource centre which will serve the whole department. Almost certainly the space will double-up as a pastoral area, and so lockable storage is generally desirable.

Modern Languages

In most comprehensive schools, French will be offered to all pupils for the first three years. Usually languages staff insist on a number of short periods, which makes for timetable complexity. The scheme outlined here is based on two 70-minute periods weekly and thus fits conveniently into the general scheme. It has also proved attractive to staff and successful with pupils.

In the first year, some pupils may arrive with experience of primary French. Where parental choice prevails a mixed set of backgrounds is likely. However, the effect of primary French is in practice so slight (as the NFER study by Burstall, 1974, has borne out), that a teacher of average resourcefulness can quickly see how to move each child forward. No written work will have been done, so recapitulation is always necessary and it is easy to take this opportunity to extend the vocabulary of pupils where appropriate. Stable links between pupil and teacher are important at this stage, and so there will be no rotation of staff unless the need for presenting all pupils with a good fluent accent makes this advisable. The object will be the acquisition of sounds and a basic vocabulary, and over the year the proportion of oral to written work will be roughly as 3 to 2. Each lesson will see about three separate activities, for example: introduction of vocabulary, using pictures; revision and practice; writing it down. About 12 new words can be learnt weekly, even by pupils who are being withdrawn for remedial help – providing their timetable of withdrawals is carefully noted by staff and taken into account.

In the second year, rotation of staff between non-streamed groups can begin after the first term. This pooling of talents is helpful and each teacher might retain a group for 2 weeks. Thus in a half-year of 3 staff to 90 pupils, the 'circus' will run for 6 weeks with all three staff on a given theme, like 'holidays'. The circus phases can be interleaved with a stable period when teacher and group stay together. Some grammar will be taught; it seems important to present verbs at this stage as the key to the language structure. But the course will be vocabulary rather than grammar-based, and a pictorial approach will be essential.

The concept of tense will be introduced in the third year, and that of the perfect tense in particular, will not be easy for perhaps 30 per cent of the year group. There are advantages in hiving off some of these in a separate group, where a course based on France and French culture can continue in French dialogue and rebuild confidence. Some of these pupils may still wish to opt for French in the fourth year, and will be given extra work if they cannot rejoin the mainstream. In the third year the services of a French assistant are particularly helpful, and the team organisation gives the flexibility needed to make the best use of this facility. The emphasis will now have shifted from vocabulary to grammar, and the proportion of oral and written work will be equal. In these three years of compulsory French, a basic course like the published Longman text will be helpful and can be adapted as necessary. But in the main, home-grown materials will be needed; pictures, stories, playscripts, and tapes. Tape facilities are best offered as flexibly as possible, which points to portable 6- or 8-outlet recorders rather than the rigidity of the language laboratory. A few in-built booths in each classroom will be most useful; but for effective learning the teacher will realise that his humanity and personality are more valuable than hardware.

Up to half the year-group will opt to continue with French as an examination subject in years 4 and 5, and mixed-ability groups can be maintained until the autumn term of the fifth year. A French exchange trip for all these pupils is valuable.

It is most likely that German will be offered as a second foreign language, and almost half the year group are likely to take this up as a single 70-minute period in a third year introductory course. The object and dative case can be tackled in the first term, and by the time of option choices at Easter pupils will have a sound idea of what German is like. Up to 20 per cent of the year-group will opt to continue with it, and O-level and CSE pupils can be kept together in the same group for both fourth and fifth years. It seems desirable that a comprehensive school should also offer Latin, since this is a course requirement at a number of universities. One answer is to provide it as a 'quickie' in the sixth form, to traditional O-level in perhaps four terms. Educationally it is, of course, much better to offer it at third year level as well as German, when the Cambridge Classics Project course may be used with good effect. In an average year, perhaps 8 out of 180 pupils might opt for it. It is therefore expensive in staffing terms, but it must be borne in mind that because our common curriculum reduces the number of option columns so effectively in years 4 and 5, the wastefulness of small option groups of 10 and 12 students is largely avoided. One can therefore afford to provide Latin, which ought not really to be regarded as a luxury subject in all conscience.

English and Expressive Arts

English is a component of humanities along with history, geography and religious education; and of expressive arts along with music and drama. Its presence in both faculties gives it a wide influence and plenty of scope, but its organisation will need to be sensitive enough to make the best use of these chances. Although there seems no reason why English could not achieve full effect in humanities alone, its presence in a grouping like expressive arts as described here would seem of benefit both to English and the other subjects involved.

In the first three years, an allocation of three (70-minute) periods to each half year means that a team of specialists in each of the three subjects can be mounted, and deployed either as a group on a combined project or as single periods weekly in each subject for each of the three non-streamed groups in the half year. The latter pattern is generally used, but for at least 6 weeks in each year a project is operated on such themes as festivals, change, and economy of expression (e.g. the rondo) in years 1, 2 and 3 respectively. And informal groupings of 2 of the 3 subjects on a week-to-week basis are common. This scheme gives English staff the continuity to pursue style and punctuation. Trays of paperbacks are circulated in each lesson from the faculty library, and rather than a textbook, English staff will use published poetry and literature cards and broadsheets along with their own materials and gramophone records. The approach in expressive arts will be thematic, with interludes for specialist skills like music notation. Themes like 'creatures' (first year) or 'stuff and nonsense' (second) will last for half a term. Compared with humanities, the work will be more flexible, and less content-bound.

The subject-period pattern is mainly preferred in years 4 and 5, alongside a convenient theme. For example, a local production of *Romeo and Juliet* might make this a good drama choice, with music links to *West Side Story*, and English exploiting social conflict. Or 'the oddball' might be taken as a theme, with English and drama using *The Snow Goose*, *St Joan* and the film *Kes*, and students composing music to illustrate the contrast between the individual as himself, as he sees himself, and as others see him. A theme of this kind can work towards a performance as the product of a learning process, and also offers opportunities for work in moral education, which is another component of expressive arts. Its role in school organisation will be discussed in the next chapter; but there is certainly scope within a faculty that links English and drama to present ME-rich situations when they arise organically from the work. In some cases it is possible to use material from the Schools Council Moral Education Project; but only because it relates to current work. If sensitivity material is used as a kind of bolt-on extra, it will not involve the pupils emotionally and may even be counter productive. It may also be possible to use, at times, materials from the Humanities Curriculum Project packs, but in general these are overloaded with wordy extracts from sources like the *Spectator*. And certainly the project's recommended mode of discussion using a 'neutral chairman' would be inappropriate to a common curriculum where the teacher is in authority, in the sense that he knows rather more about the world than a pupil can and is respected for making this clear. Indeed, this 'holy ground' between teacher and pupil, in Lawrence's phrase, gives a potential gradient across which knowledge flows. But the teacher will not want to stuff his opinion down his pupils' throats; rather will he allow them to work out their own views, but stand up and be counted himself when – as will inevitably happen – he is asked to say what he thinks. The pupils need not accept his view; but they will know him as a person, and give his view the weight of his character and experience. That would seem to be something they have a right to.

Drama is a valuable component of a compulsory five-year course where, as here, it links with cognate subjects. In working on a theme like 'loyalty', for example, staff will set up initial ideas, and then pupils will be led to produce their own, and develop an understanding of themselves and their relations with others through mime, role-play and discussion. Drama links well, too, with English as an oral skill; pupils can easily be led to talk, without knowing it, for five minutes about a new topic – for example, by establishing a mock auction where objects can be accurately described. Drama in an interrelated course can promote self-knowledge and self-confidence across the whole ability range.

Physical Activities

There are advantages here in separating games and recreational activities from physical education. The former can conveniently be blocked out across the whole year group, with the PE specialists leading a team of 6 to 10 staff, depending on timetable availability, for 5 to 6 forms of entry. The emphasis in the first two years may well be on acquiring a knowledge of basic popular games and sports. After all, at most junior schools rounders and some swimming, with football for boys and perhaps netball for girls, will be all pupils have experienced. There seems little justification for narrowing the choice of games played on a school basis in the comprehensive by concentrating on one of them as the focus of the school's prestige. Former grammar schools seem to find it difficult to extend their horizons beyond rugby football in many cases; there is no reason why excellence should not be attempted in other games too, and it makes far more sense for a comprehensive school to allocate each term to a non-exclusive emphasis on a particular game, or group of games. This can usually be agreed on an area basis with consequent mutual advantage. By the fourth and fifth years, a wider pattern of choice can extend to orienteering and sailing as staff, cost and available facilities allow.

One period weekly of games, and of PE, is in line with normal provision. For the PE the half-year group is a better unit, with between 2 and 4 staff for 75 to 90 pupils. The organisation here will depend very much on the school's facilities, but possible spaces will be a gymnasium, a swimming pool, outside areas, classrooms and a lecture theatre. With an eye to seasons and the weather, programmes can be devised which offer a rotation of activities within the 70-minute period, and which will fulfil the usual pattern of objectives that specialist staff will have in mind. In addition, inter-faculty cooperation can be established with drama in expressive arts in relation to movement skills, and with humanities and science staff in health education topics. These might be an effective component of the physical education programme from the third year onwards, and an option element in the fourth and fifth year can have appeal for older girls who show a reluctance to join in games and sports, other than a narrow range where facilities may be restricted.

Assessment and Evaluation

It will have been noticed that in all faculties, a suppleness and opportunism characterises the teacher's construction of his interface with the pupil. In a more static mode, assessment is merely a matter of recording marks, and evaluation perhaps seen as little more than choosing the right textbooks. The mode described here is more fluid and more exciting, and seems likely to be more effective. But it means a correspondingly different approach to assessment and evaluation, and to the way the teacher sees himself and his role in the school. The latter aspects will be discussed in the next chapter.

Assessment will, in some faculties, be an essential part of the work week by week. This is so in mathematics, for example, where closer control ensures there are no lacunae in a pupil's grasp of key concepts. But in any case a formal system of assessment must be devised, so that a record of a pupil's progress with each teacher can be kept centrally and made available to all staff. Such a system will also be the basis of reports to parents, which will be discussed in Chapter 9.

Experience suggests that a simple system, in which an assessment card for each pupil is raised in each faculty and filed in the staff room, gives most scope for individual variation by faculty or by teacher. Sheets of card of about A4 size can be punched for ring binding, and colour-coded for each of the 5 or 6 tutor groups in a year. Each side is pre-printed with name, form and subject, and columns headed for: topic; date begun and ended; a large space for comment;

and initials. Rather than specify sub-headings for the teacher's comment, it is better for the head of each faculty to discuss guidelines with his team and then brief staff as they join. Elaborate records with headings like 'manner, keenness, initiative, appearance, leadership, academic potential, dependability, cooperativeness' (an actual example) seem an admission that no one knows the child well enough to talk about him; and in any case, completing such a matrix with a letter from a five-point scale for each attribute really conveys no information worth putting into words. There is no substitute for actually sitting down and writing about a child, as you see him. You have to think about him and summarise your insights, and you present them in a form which tells a story to other staff.

When each pupil enters the school, the staff secretary or year tutor will head up seven cards of the kind described for each pupil, corresponding to the seven faculties. The cards are then bound up by faculty, but can easily be sorted by colour into teaching groups if required. As a rule, a requirement that at least one entry per faculty per child is made each term will ensure that assessments are regular and not rushed. A law of diminishing returns operates, since staff are only human. To ask for more frequent entries will mean they are forgotten or skimped. But in practice, two or three entries will be made by faculty decision each term where good sense suggests this is advisable. For example, a term of active project work and rotation in expressive arts may well mean a separate entry for music, English and drama. Rather than over-legislate, one can depend upon the professional conscience of staff in such matters.

Such assessments will be as full and frank as the teacher can make them, and will, of course, reflect the appraisal he has made of the child's response for the period under review, as established from written and oral work. It is likely that his comments on the pupil's books will amount to correction, and a comment; these will be more helpful, and more encouraging, than a bald mark scrawled through a forest of ticks or crosses. The point is the same as with pupil records; numerical assessments tell such a tiny part of the story. They can mislead able pupils into taking it easy, and depress a pupil with learning difficulties who may have worked much harder to achieve far less. I remember an art teacher telling me of a conversation he had with a boy whose work on a creative activities project was slow. When asked what he was writing in his project diary, the boy coloured and said he was 'trying to make it interesting'. The practical work on the project was excellent, but the boy had reading difficulties which made it hard for him to get his thoughts down on paper. The teacher quickly realised this, and the boy sensed his sympathetic response. There are bound to be subjective elements in this process of discussion and appreciation and it is important that staff are encouraged to exchange views on the basis of their judgments. Pupils often know themselves better than teachers realise. They do not expect to be overrated; but each piece of work a child produces is personal to him, and a true assessment will show an understanding of that as well as of the absolute standards it must be measured against.

The set of seven assessment cards across all faculties will give an informative picture of a pupil's work and involvement. But the teacher's process of assessment is revealing too about the learning programme itself. As the old saw has it, teachers write reports on themselves. When the teacher is himself selecting and organising learning experiences, evaluation of their effect must be a part of the process. He will be looking all the time at the pupils' responses, and will take steps to ensure that worksheets and textbooks do not get in the way of this interpretive role. He will need to be honest with himself, and ask himself how much he admits he has recognised in their responses. It will help to get pupils themselves talking about a project. For some teachers, their appraisal will in the end be a gut reaction; for others, it will be the result of a cumulative sequence of individual judgments, made while the work is in progress, and comparing educational outcomes against criteria derived from professional skills and the school's whole strategy. In some faculties, diagnostic tests can be set more easily than in others; but independent checks of this kind, which are all of a piece with the work in hand, will always be helpful and are preferable to formal examinations in the first three years.

The important thing, then, about curriculum evaluation is that it must always be seen as an organic part of curriculum development. It has become a fashionable topic of late, and there are few pieces of school-based innovation which, at first blush, can resist the researcher's inquiry 'But what about evaluation?' Certainly it is meet and right that we must be reminded about it. Recent work on such concepts as illuminative evaluation is also helpful, and has exposed the serious deficiencies of psychometric approaches. Yet, at the end of the day, we are back with the teacher in the school, and all that happens is only of value in so far as it can help him to see evaluation as part of curriculum process; that is, as a part of his role in the whole school. Micro-approaches, where individual teachers are 'triangulated' by examining the responses of teacher, observer and pupil are really missing the point; it is the whole set of values, styles and intentions in the school which will determine the context and the transaction. And to argue that the task of illuminative evaluation is to examine these factors is to go round in a circle, which ultimately can be broken only by asking the teacher how he sees it. In the next chapter these aspects will get further consideration.

In short, the link between assessment of pupil or teacher, and evaluation of the learning system, will be the curriculum; and this in turn will be a function of the school's philosophy, or lack of it. This is tacitly assumed when parents are invited, at school speech days, to admire external examination results. The peculiarity of the English and Welsh maintained school is that it is part of a national system, locally administered; and thus enjoys remarkable autonomy. The price the school pays might, not unreasonably, be considered to be its subjection to external examinations at 16 plus, which European schools are spared in return for a greater degree of central control. No examinations are welcome; but to see O-level and CSE as a barrier to innovation is both untrue, as I hope to have shown, and unwise. For if the new approaches work, they will enhance pupil performance; and it is not difficult to choose or design examinations which reflect, rather than determine, the curriculum. We must never forget that exam results tell us about only a part of a student's attitudes and accomplishments today, and nothing about his achievements tomorrow. But it is folly not to value them for what they are, and to realise that when they are good, they will reassure parents and thus give a positive boost to curriculum development. They may well in part reflect the growing certainty and confidence with which new approaches are implemented. In this respect, it is worth tabulating some results for the first three years of 16 plus examinations at Sheredes School:

TABLE 4·1

	1976	1975	1974
Proportion of candidates in year group obtaining at least one subject grade	100%	98%	96%
Proportion obtaining 5 or more O-level or CSE subjects (all grades)	92%	88%	75%
Proportion obtaining 3 or more O-level (grades A, B, C) or CSE grade 1	42%	31%	26%
Average number of subject grades per student in whole year group	7.1	6.6	5.4

There is a tendency for schools simply to quote subject pass rates, and these are almost meaningless since only clever candidates may have been entered. A general recognition of the value of results on a year-group basis would be helpful to parents.

I am suggesting that even the present divided 16 plus system of O-level and CSE is not inimical to curriculum innovation. But the recent enthusiasm displayed by the odd alliance of politicians, DES and LEA representatives for tests that will 'monitor educational performance' may well turn out to be another matter. The philosophy of this exercise has been summarised by Kay (1975), who has been associated with the work of the DES Assessment of Performance Unit. In an article in which he admits that 'My purpose is more to initiate discussion than to suggest solutions – I raise more questions than I seek to answer', he queries whether it would be both desirable and possible to assess pupil performance by a system of national tests, based not on subject diversity but on what he terms 'lines of development'. In mathematics, for example, he lists communication through number, graph, model and diagram. But he confesses that:

> none of these lines of development can be isolated from a context of knowledge . . . the form in which they exist may be markedly changed by the subject matter with which they are associated. . . . Is it . . . possible to assess the degree to which the aims are being met without dictating content?

One can only share his doubts. The difficulties of this kind of testing have been specified by Hamilton (1976): 'To produce achievement tests would almost certainly focus too much attention on particular items of knowledge at the expense of more general processes of learning.' He goes on to quote Stake's experience of these approaches in the USA:

> Most state accountability proposals call for more uniform standards across the state, greater pre-specification of objectives, more careful analysis of learning sequences, and better testing of student performances. . . . What they bring is more bureaucracy, more subterfuge, and more constraint on student opportunities to learn.

Stake's comments were written in 1973. It seems all too likely that once again we shall have the worst aspects of American experience thrust upon us. For, of course, there is the basic objection that performance tests, unless virtually trivial, cannot be separated from curriculum content, and will therefore influence it. But what may be more serious is the inhibiting effect the tests might easily have on a climate of change. Performance tests offer a ready-made reason for sticking to traditional lines and, unlike O-level and CSE, they may well penetrate the 11–16 curriculum at the ages of 11, 13 and 15. To see these years as a five-year continuum will be made even harder than at present. Even if they finally emerge, as is quite likely given the inherent logical difficulties, in severely attenuated form, the tests will impose a further constraint and an extended bureaucracy. Heads and teachers must watch this development with the greatest attention, and be unswerving in a commitment to education for its own sake. There is all the more reason to look closely, critically and urgently at curriculum design, and develop a coherent rationale which will win for a school a broad base of commonsense support.

Chapter 5

Action and Implementation:

Styles of Deliberation and Management

It was quite a long time ago that Broudy, Smith and Burnett (1964) wrote of the school as a 'total influence system'. They regard the secondary school as the pivot of education, because it 'mediates between the potentialities of childhood and the actualities of adulthood'. And they see it not as 'providing numerous, different programs in order that everyone can get *some* kind of education' but a common education, in which different ability levels are met by 'adjusting the sophistication and detail of what is taught'. But, as we have seen, practical illustrations of these aims are thin on the ground; there are many influences which can frustrate the implementation of a curriculum design. In this chapter I want to look at styles of action and decision in the school, with reference to two aspects: the influence of these styles, for the pupil, in promoting moral and social education; and their influence, for the teacher, in making the school a place where curriculum change can be sustained.

The view of school as a 'total influence system' is one that would have been shared by Thring of Uppingham who, as a pioneering headmaster of the English public school, recognised that all the aspects of the school experienced by the boy should reinforce the school's aims. But it is evident from Thring's remark, 'I am supreme here and will brook no interference', that developing those aims was essentially a one-man show. It is surprising, though, that a recent study by Bernbaum (1975) suggests that headmasters still see their task in a traditional and highly personal way, and that there is no 'widespread translation of the traditional perspectives relating to the role into a view which might lie within a framework of administrative theory or bureaucratic rules.' Yet we have seen that curriculum design must be very much a collaborative exercise. Does it follow that any suggestion of *force majeure* or separate decision-making must be detached from the head's role? Bernbaum's study suggests that such a change would be revolutionary rather than evolutionary. And in any case, evolution is all we need. There is no reason why patterns of leadership and participation should be mutually exclusive, and every reason for devising systems in which they can coexist. For the leader can initiate strategies, settle issues and rationalise action in a way a committee cannot; and teachers instinctively recognise this when they elect, as they invariably do, a leader for a curriculum team. As for the head's role, Hoyle (1975) observes:

> There is little doubt that innovation owes much to the most progressive of British head teachers. The question must be asked whether the same initiative can be given by the collective leadership of teachers or whether self-cancelling 'veto groups' might not inhibit innovation.

But if the initiative and drive of the head are essential, so also will be the commitment and understanding of staff. We, therefore, need guidelines for a path between the extremes of autocracy and collectivism, and one which will lead us to a workable way of promoting and controlling change.

There is another reason why we should move in this direction. To view school as a total influence system is to recognise that it is possible to make it more than the sum of its component parts. For Thring, it made the inculcation of manliness and godliness more effective; for us, it makes the common curriculum a cultural artefact rather than a collection of school subjects. On the face of it, such a system could the more readily become an instrument of indoctrination. It is evident, for example, from a recent study of Dartington Hall School (Punch, 1977) that even a society committed to openness and pupil participation develops its own control mechanisms. There are two points to be made here. First, even an unplanned curriculum, like the familiar pattern of fourth- and fifth-year multiple options, exerts a biasing effect; the NFER research quoted in Chapter 2 shows how less-able pupils do less well out of it and develop changed attitudes. Second, any attempt at coherent curriculum planning is open to such a charge, and it is a further reason why it is important to seek a broad base for an innovation programme, as I have argued in Chapter 3, and to ensure that curriculum and organisation decisions are made in the same spirit. The process of decision-making therefore deserves attention.

We can look at this problem both strategically and structurally. It is useful to bear in mind the well-known typology of innovation strategies due to Bennis, Benne and Chin (1969):

Power-coercive strategies involve the use of legal or administrative power;
Empirical-rational strategies assume that people will respond best to rational explanation;
Normative-reeducative strategies assume that innovation requires changes of attitude and imply a change agent.

Skilbeck (1976), in an analysis of school-based development, suggests there might be power-coercive allocation of staff to key roles; normative-re-educative efforts by change agents to bring about in participants a changed perception of tasks, and rational-empirical appeals to research data and theory on uses of assessment procedures. This proposal is based on what Skilbeck terms a rational-interactive model of curriculum development, where decisions are shared by a wider range of participants than in a 'rational-deductive' model, which he suggests is appropriate in a centrally dominated curriculum system, where 'the essential curriculum task of the school is to interpret central directives to the satisfaction of the controllers . . .'. His third model, intuitive decision-making, stresses 'immediate judgment by teachers, spontaneity . . . the individual classroom becomes the centre of decision-making.' He suggests that the rational – interactive model deserves support:

> Teachers have a more complex role . . . and have more demands made on them . . . teachers need new knowledge, skills and attitudes. . . . These skills include reflective self-criticism and cooperative group work. . . . The model also requires headteachers and other traditional authority figures to relinquish some of their power and to learn to share responsibility.

This is a helpful model although, as Skilbeck points out, decision-making in practice is something of a mixture of all three types and we shall return to the creative aspects of the intuitive model.

Theoretical analysis of this kind starts with an understanding of what schools are like. This is not so with administrative theory which attempts to take management and behaviourist concepts and apply them to schools. A ubiquitous and pernicious form is systems theory, which sees all organisations in a context of environment, and individuals' functions as exchanges with this environment. The difficulty is that the sorts of exchanges in as complex a process as teaching and learning cannot be satisfactorily operationalised; but this does not deter the devotees of this approach, which is currently prominent in management thinking, from attempting to foist it onto schools. Its implication is that school organisation starts from specifying roles and tasks; from this the structures can be established. Doubtless this is a good way of administering a municipal crematorium, where the tasks are simple and the roles easily defined; although already one can see that the concept of boundaries is so prominent as to repress initiative and promote needless demarcations. But it makes little sense in a school, where the structure, as we have seen, must come from a fundamental analysis of education and curriculum.

Systems theory is on all fours with the behavioural objectives model of curriculum planning discussed in Chapter 3. It is as irrelevant to studying a school's work as the objectives model is misleading to teachers devising learning experiences. But schools must be on their guard against ill-conceived attempts to apply it to them. Thus, a systems objective might be 'to achieve meaningful relationships', and a positive performance indicator would be 'common room activities on and off site, in and out of working hours'; a negative indicator would be 'incidence of union meetings' (Bolton and Richardson, 1976). The fatuity of this approach might not be so evident to administrators fresh from management courses. Indeed, the elaborate listing of 'management tasks' in order to specify the precise roles of senior staff has gained some popularity with heads lately, and although it is helpful to know at least what people are doing, the exercise runs the same risks as the objectives model in curriculum planning. It is essentially closed; it is prescriptive rather than interpretive.

It is important for heads to know the concerns of their masters, and management concepts are to blame for the theory of corporate management which – having been largely discredited by industry in the late 1960s – has been embraced by local government and is proving most damaging to the education service. Harrison's (1976) analysis here is instructive. He points out its derivation from a Weberian view of rational bureaucracy, and accounts for its popularity in local government, in over-centralising management, by the fact that this 'all too neatly coincides with controlling political tendencies'. The basic error is that the common management of resources is not the same as the common management of services, of which education is so important. The lesson of all this, for schools, is to devise ways of moving decision-making away from the centre, but in such a way that the piece of the action that is passed to the head of department or the teacher is a piece he can handle.

This brings us to structural ways of tackling this problem, and suggests a useful approach by specifying criteria for participation. It is reasonable to propose, as a general principle, that decision-making should be moved from the centre to the periphery, but subject to three conditions. First, that the body or individual to whom the decision is delegated, is in possession of all the information needed to make a rational decision; second, that consideration must be given to the extent to which it or he bears responsibility for that decision; and third, that schools are places where expediency may call for a speedy, central decision in order to resolve an unexpected problem. Thus, the internal appointment of a new year tutor would lie with the head, who will have an independent view of each candidate's relations with staff, pupils and parents, as well as an appreciation of his professional effectiveness; and ultimately he bears responsibility for the appointment as the agent of the governing body. But a decision as to whether uniform rules should be relaxed in certain circumstances in school would be one for all the staff, since every teacher will have the responsibility of enforcing it, and all can be briefed on the issues underlying it. Similarly, decisions on the allocation of general allowance funds between faculties, or the schedule for parents' evenings throughout the year, should be taken by heads of faculties along with year tutors. There are likely to be a number of decisions of this latter type, and this procedure could be institutionalised by regular meetings of the head and deputies, heads of faculty and year tutors as a body.

Such a body suffers, though, from the disadvantage that even though its minutes may be displayed in the staff room and its agenda open, staff can feel that their involvement in important decisions is not adequately represented by the transmission of their concerns from faculty meetings via heads of faculty. One solution is to extend full membership of the body on a rotational basis to all the staff, in turn. Thus, to the head and two deputies in a 5- or 6-form entry school, the seven heads of faculty along with the heads of careers and English and the coordinator of remedial studies, and the six year tutors, one would add for each meeting three staff taken from an alphabetical list of those holding some post of responsibility not previously represented, and three from a similar list of those remaining. This would give a conveniently sized body of about 23 people, and with three or four meetings a term all staff would attend it in the course of the year. This, the Pastakorg Committee, would be responsible for pastoral and academic organisation, and the extended membership gives all staff the opportunity to take part in the discussion and resolution of decisions, and easy access if they wish a particular point of view to be put forward.

Certain decisions, then, will be made by the head, possibly in conjunction with his deputies as a management team. A study reported by Musgrove (1971) shows that this is in keeping with teachers views, who 'approved of the head taking decisions by himself' on a surprisingly wide range of issues, and a wider one than is suggested here: including the rules of behaviour for pupils; what is taught in the school; and how often parents and the public are invited to school. But:

> They wished to be consulted over . . . responsibility allowances; teachers' timetables; the selection of teaching aids . . . and the type of report form used. In short, they wished to extend the range of issues with which the headmaster is concerned; and they wished to be consulted over a larger

number of issues; but they saw a number of key matters as being the headmaster's sole concern.

The scope of a committee of the Pastakorg type makes it possible to go further than this in many respects, and this would indeed be necessary if the school is to be the focus of rational-interactive planning. In addition to faculty meetings and year meetings, weekly meetings of the year tutors might be conducted by one of the deputies, with general responsibility for pastoral organisation. This facilitates the devolving of many pastoral decisions onto year tutors and is in line with the policy of getting decision-making as close as possible to the problem. The Pastakorg Committee would, of course, coopt the heads of music and drama to a meeting where, say, school productions were discussed; and at the annual meeting to hammer out an agreed allocation of funds between faculties, other staff with responsibility for finance would attend. This would include the library and the central resource fund, which conveniently includes materials and services to do with the reprographic centre and basic stationery needs. Specialist needs (like squared paper for mathematics) would be a faculty responsibility. And the option of additional *ad hoc* committees is a useful one when a new or occasional matter enters the arena; perhaps a new curriculum initiative, or perhaps deciding the best way of distributing money raised by a sponsored swim.

A stratified but adaptable system of decision-making of this kind preserves an element of leadership as directed authority in the relations between staff at the various levels of responsibility, but also gives a rational basis for their involvement in decision and discussion so as to initiate and energise their commitment to the school's strategies. These are all formal meetings, but it would be unlikely if each at every level were recorded as written minutes. A close control must be kept of the amount of paper circulating. Too much, and little gets read; and writing things down loses nuances and shifts emphases. Also, the formality of the written word can render rigid a discussion which all involved might have seen in terms of open options. On the other hand, written records of the transactions of key committees can be valuable.

It is sometimes suggested that general staff meetings are a proper forum for discussion of all topics. This is a collectivist stance, and likely to be inspired by political rather than educational considerations. Experience of such meetings soon shows that discussion falls into the hands of a few teachers, who enjoy talking and are anxious to offer views on every subject. Furthermore, good talkers are not necessarily good doers, or good thinkers. There are many hard-working, dedicated teachers who want to 'get on with it', and whose contributions to such meetings rarely have the force of those who are more practised at advocacy. In any case, there is only time for a few contributions, if the meetings are not to be seen as endless after-school chores; in which case, only the activists will attend. The objections recently voiced by union representatives to the DES 'great debate' meetings in the country apply with the same force to any meeting where a complex issue is to be discussed by upwards of 40 people. And teachers have only a limited amount of time for after-school activities; an innovating school will not get very far if it does not allow teachers to lead full and active private lives, as other professional people do. It follows that talk is a valuable commodity, to be shared among the conflicting claims of after-school games and clubs, meetings of year teams, trips to the teachers' centre and – perhaps most valuable of all – informal conversation not about doctrine, ideology and teacher politics but about pupils, what they learn and how they learn. This is most likely to happen when a structure for decision-making gives staff the security of knowing where they stand and how they are involved.

This secure feeling is essential if teachers are to do their best work, and it is quickly communicated to pupils. Indeed, what is sauce for the goose in staff relations, is sauce for the gander in staff-pupil relations. We can now turn to look at the ways in which pupils, too, can be involved in the school's affairs so as to fulfil tasks in social and moral education mentioned earlier. We can distinguish a number of contributory elements. First will be the way in which a harmonious style of cooperation and teamwork among teachers gives an exemplar to pupils of productive social interaction without confrontation. The emphasis will be on respect arising not from a person's status or talents as such, but from the way the use of those talents promotes the common good. This applies with equal force to heads. The head who insists that pupils must stand when he walks into a classroom is indicating that his status is more important than the pupils getting on, uninterrupted, with their work. He will gain far more respect, and therefore effectiveness, by having lunch every day with his pupils, talking to them about their interests and schoolwork and thus demonstrating to them – by action, not just words – that he considers their views important. In these matters, the head and staff must set an example which runs directly counter to the styles of effectiveness given so much prominence in the media; of walk-outs, disputes, exhortatory letters from management to workers, and unreasoning conflict by workers towards management. These are everyday signs of rock-bottom relationships. It is to be hoped that when schools are urged, as at present, to acquaint their pupils with what industry is like, schools do not allow their enthusiasm to run away with them.

Next, we must recognise the potent influence a non-streamed format has for social and moral goals. Although non-streaming has been justified here solely in terms of curriculum aims, there is no doubt that the quality of understanding between pupils is vastly enhanced. The atmosphere, the 'feel' of a school that is non-streamed for the right reasons has about it a mixture of tough-mindedness and relaxation, of directness and sensitivity that a visitor can spot in twenty minutes. But there is nothing soft about it; fairness and tolerance do not exclude competitiveness and hard work.

Another profound force for social and moral education will be the implicit adoption by the school of a consistent set of civilised values. If staff display honesty, trust and a respect for others in their dealings with themselves and pupils they are transmitting signals which pupils will pick up and which will be mutually reinforcing. This is not a matter of religious belief; they are values which will be shared alike by Christian and humanist. And this is important, because inconsistency by staff does great damage to a civilised community. In a staff versus pupils football match, for example, a teacher must not allow his desire to score to lead him to act unreasonably towards other staff or pupils; and if both boys and girls are to be addressed by staff by their first names (which would seem, *pace* recent legislation, a minimal requirement in a civilised mixed school) it matters that all staff do it. The teacher is not a private tutor, setting his own personal code of organisation and behaviour; he is a member of a team, enjoying great autonomy but accepting the values of the community in the construction of which he is, by the same token, invited to take part.

All these aspects are important. But what is still missing is a mechanism which formally recognises that schools exist for pupils, and that pupils will sense a greater engagement if they have opportunities to put over their view of school. It would be a great error to misconstrue this as arguing for the direct involvement of pupils with curriculum planning. Their indirect involvement with the organisation of learning is another matter, and in the previous chapter I have stressed its importance as part of the evaluative process staff will adopt. A specific example will help. It is necessary that the teachers planning a piece of work in the third-year French course take account of pupil reactions to similar work, so as to make it as effective as possible. And it is desirable that pupils who cannot see the point of third-year French have a mechanism which will allow them, without rancour, to explain their view and to expect also a considered reply. But it is quite another thing to suggest that third-year pupils should vote on whether or not the French course should continue.

It is unfortunate that the clamant advocacy of collectivism by educationists with Marxist and similar leanings should make it necessary to distinguish the latter view; for it flies so patently in the face of common sense and can have no place in a concept of schooling as an intentional process of initiation into the culture. Well-meaning attempts have been made to take an eccentric view of democracy and run schools on the basis of such 'moots'. But the risk is considerable that, whatever the intention, the result will be to frustrate the purpose of school as a place where, as Oakeshott has put it (1972), a pupil is 'acquiring in some measure an understanding of a human condition in which the "fact of life" is continuously illuminated by a "quality of life".'

We return to the task of outlining a mechanism which will give pupils the opportunities we should like to offer. If we take a representative form of democracy as a basis, then each form or pastoral group might elect a boy and a girl to the 'school forum' each term. The forum should meet weekly in school time, to match its importance in the school, and the chair could be taken by year tutors on a rotating basis. It is convenient to have one such forum for, say, the first three years, and another for the fourth and fifth years. This takes account of growing maturity and prevents unwieldy numbers. Each week in form time pupils can then put forward topics for forum discussion, and it should be possible to conduct it in a place where pupils may themselves attend as observers. Then in a subsequent session in the form, the form's representatives can give an account of what happened and initiate discussion. Each week's agenda would consist of matters arising, plus new matters raised on the spot. Other year tutors would attend, along with any staff who were interested.

To take the example previously given, a pupil from the third year would raise the question of French in his form, and this would in turn be raised by one of the form representatives at the forum. The chairman would probably suggest that next week, the head of languages would be invited to come along and talk about French as a part of the third-year curriculum. And at that subsequent meeting, it might be that the head or his deputy, who might well attend each meeting, would then ask the tutor in the chair if he could add his own comments on languages as a compulsory curriculum element. In this way pupils can be given an insight into curriculum decisions, and feel that although in this case French is here to stay, all the same they have been put in the picture.

On the other hand, the question of providing an additional drinking fountain may be brought up. Possibly the need for this may have escaped the notice of staff, and the head would recognise it as a valuable suggestion to put to the LEA, for attention as soon as maintenance facilities allow. Or a new way of organising the queue for school dinners might be proposed, and be well worth looking at. A suggestion for, say, a first- and second-year disco could lead to the setting up of a forum committee to organise it.

A forum of this kind gives pupils the chance to understand also how democratic processes work; and this seems an important way in which schools should prepare pupils for society. And if the forum representatives in turn keep the minutes, it might well be possible to have them typed up and exhibited on the forum space on the school notice board.

Forum business will be transacted in a cool, civilised and rather informal style; the chairman will expect silence and politeness, but the atmosphere of the council chamber would be inhibiting.

In some ways, the forum complements the traditional school assembly, which many heads still see as a powerful social and moral force. The work of the Schools Council Moral Education Project has, however, shown that its moral role can be greatly overrrated. And as a religious device, it has been recognised by church authorities in several instances as virtually a counter-productive influence. Undoubtedly religious education, on the lines I have already discussed, is an essential curriculum element; but I am equally certain that the morning 'act of worship' may be positive inoculation against pupils taking a sympathetic view of man's need for religious faith. At best, it will leave pupils cold. But assemblies serve two other important functions. Socially, they have a cohesive effect on the school. This must not be overstressed, and certainly does not justify whole school assemblies every day. But it does suggest that an assembly once a week for years 1, 2 and 3, and for years 4, 5 and 6, along with a weekly year assembly, will be helpful. This would then for each pupil take up two of the five weekly morning sessions before the first lesson, leaving room for forum, and forum feedback, to take up two and one over for, perhaps, school-dinner tickets and the school bank, trip money and similar matters; as well as the continuing pastoral work with the form tutor.

School assembly also introduces pupils to the idea of the formal occasion, which is an important part of our culture, whether it be a marriage service or an annual general meeting. Given these two rather different objectives, it makes sense to relate the content of assembly to a wider pattern than a hymn, a homily and a prayer. It can be seen in part as a showcase for curriculum work, particularly from a faculty like expressive arts; it can be used for musical items by talented pupils, or the collective curriculum work of pupils; and it can be an opportunity for any member of staff to talk about an enthusiasm or experience. It can be a chance, too, to bring in outside speakers on a theme of special interest or topicality. Year assemblies can be devised by form tutors in turn, using the talents of each form.

We have looked at ways in which the relations between staff, and the relations of staff with pupils, can set a style of civilised intercourse which derives from and further advances both the school's curriculum aims and the ways in which staff can sustain them. But we must now look more closely at the actual management of curriculum innovation and see if we can clarify further the role of the school as the focus for curriculum development. Let us see first what we can learn from management in industry, bearing in mind the defects and dangers Taylor (1973) specifies in making parallels between the management of schools and of a commercial or industrial enterprise:

> First, they fail to bring out the real and essential differences between educational considerations and market considerations. This is not to say there is nothing in common between running a commercial enterprise and running a large school. Problems of control and delegation, of communication and departmental autonomy, of bureaucracy and budget determination are common. . . . But . . . the analogy . . . fails to take account of certain characteristics of the values inherent in a market structure as compared to those characteristic of educational structures.

Taylor goes on to quote Jules Henry: 'In the market the anchorage of value is always on the self; the anchorage in human relations is always on the other.' His second objection is that the analogy encourages us to think of the 'them' and 'us' style of management and labour. And third, seeing the head's role in management terms encourages us to legitimate his role by his skills as a manager and not 'by his stature as educator'. These are important reservations and effectively limit the usefulness of the parallel to the communication, delegation and administration aspects Taylor has identified; and we have already discussed all three to some extent.

In a recent study, the government-sponsored Training Services Agency has outlined three essential skills needed in a manager. First comes the knowledge relevant to the job, such as financial and marketing know-how, which the agency feels is met by the existing apparatus of business schools and management courses. For the teacher, this need is filled partly by pre-service subject and professional training, and partly by in-service courses away from the school, in teachers' centres and other places. Second are the skills of analytical problem-solving, decision-making and communicating expertise; and third comes the ability for the manager to go on learning. The agency suggests that Britain is far from successful at fulfilling the second and third aims and, according to a report in the *Sunday Times* of 13.2.77, 'suggests that using the real problems of the organisation as learning opportunities could be a way forward here'.

This conclusion really only echoes the view that has already been advanced here; that in an innovating school, the learning process extends to the teachers as well. On the whole, we may conclude that industry can teach us little about this vital area, and that we are as much on our own in investigating it as we ever were. But this is not quite the case, for it has been found that problem-solving skills, or 'trouble shooting', are the main job of the manager in industry, and can be much improved by inviting him to change jobs with managers in other enterprises facing different problems. The technique, which is called Action Learning, recognises also that 'learning is a social process and that people gain more from group interchange, debate, and if necessary disagreement, than from working in isolation.' This is a familiar argument to us, since it is a recognised benefit of faculty organisation into staff teams. And although there is everything to be said for a more flexible career structure in education, which would make it possible for the head of faculty in a school to change places, say, with the head of department in a further education institution for a term, it is not easy to see how the general notion of job-swapping will advance the kinds of problem-solving skills faced by a teacher in a curriculum team.

But the interesting aspect of this technique is its emphasis on what Schwab (1964) has called 'the practical disciplines [of] choice, decision and action based on deliberate decision', rather than the theoretical disciplines which, in this case, are represented by the prescriptions and researches of the management schools, and which have evidently been singularly unsuccessful in improving skills in two management areas which are directly apposite to skills we wish to develop in teachers. So that although we cannot expect to solve our problem by exchanging a mathematics teacher with a history teacher, we cannot fail to take note of the simple means that is successfully achieving an end which all the fancy management theories have failed to reach.

Let us look next at a proposal Stenhouse (1975) has made to determine the role of the teacher in school-based curriculum development. In his 'research model', he finds it necessary 'to cast the developer not in the role of creator or man with a mission, but in that of the investigator. The curriculum he creates . . . is conceived as a probe through which to explore and test hypotheses and not as a recommendation to be adopted.' He argues for:

> the development of a tradition in evaluation which is research oriented in that it aims at understanding rather than merely judgement of merit. It seems possible to build on the experience gained in this tradition by letting the evaluation, as it were, lead the curriculum rather than follow it. The curriculum would be designed with its potential contribution to research strongly in mind . . . it would have the function of a research probe.

To be sure, Stenhouse is right in seeking to eliminate the distinction between curriculum development and curriculum evaluation which characterises the process model. But when he writes:

> I take the view that curriculum development should be handled as educational research. The developer should be an investigator rather than a reformer. He should start from a problem, not from a solution. And he should not aim to be right, but to be competent . . .

it is difficult not to raise an eybrow at this picture of the teacher not as creator or reformer, but as researcher and investigator. It seems to see the task of the teacher as one in which all is problematic, and where 'what we ask of a curriculum offering is not that it should be right or good but that it should be intelligent and penetrating'. This seems to discount the place of value judgments. And my experience in developing a school-based curriculum programme suggests that even the most talented and resilient teacher would be surprised, if not dismayed, to learn that the test we would all apply to his offering would be to ask whether it was intelligent or penetrating. For teachers have beliefs; they have optimism; and they have heart. More than anything they want to develop a curriculum which they can consider is right and good.

I am at pains, though, less to criticise the perceptive and sympathetic analysis Stenhouse makes of these issues than to stress what seem to me to be the mainsprings of the teacher's drive to innovate. Yet it is hard not to feel that the research model is wrong logically, as well as psychologically. The bloodless, neutral skills of the researcher are at the opposite pole from the reasoning passion and creative intuition of the innovating teacher. He will, as Stenhouse recognises, evaluate what he does largely while he is doing it; but when the team gets together to appraise their work, they will do so not with the backward glance of the researcher, nit-picking at imagined pseudo-problems; they will look forward to a new strategy with the positive intuition and awareness of the man who has created something good, and now wants to get on with the task of creating something better. If the team have tried their hardest, that's that. They know, without having to discuss it, that it was their best but that it wasn't good enough. But they are all a little older and a little wiser. So it's worth trying again.

The research model, in short, fails chiefly because, in basing its rationale on the theoretical rather than the practical disciplines, it misunderstands the innovating process. And we have seen before that this preoccupation in curriculum with an extraneous but superficially respectable theoretic can be seriously misleading. As Schwab puts it: 'We have tended to fall into the habit of treating all disciplines proper to the schools as if they were theoretical.' Strictly, theoretical disciplines will be those whose subject matters are such that the knowledge these disciplines seek will be as nearly stable as knowledge can be. But in education, as Warnock (1973) has observed, the whole subject is practical. 'One must not, as Aristotle said, demand more rigour than the subject matter is fitted for. . . . If there are theories, they must essentially be analytic of what actually occurs.'

If we can learn anything from management in industry, it must be that the pursuit of theoretical models for such a complex and practical process as innovating in education will generate a lot of work for the researchers but throw precious little light on the world of action. If we go a bit further with the *creative action* model that has emerged from this discussion, we may get a better picture of how school-based innovation can be sustained. We have the idea of the teacher who will derive great strength from being part of a creative team, and who will seek to interpret the school's curriculum strategy in terms of a learning system. He will have a set of criteria in mind which will, as it were, set the scene for his programme; but he will exercise his intuition along with his specialist skills, and he will finally, with his colleagues, put the programme into action. And only then will he really know what it is like.

We can draw two parallels with this process from two very different professional activities. The analogy between curriculum and engineeering as examples of action sciences has been mentioned in Chapter 1. The field of curriculum draws on philosophy, sociology, psychology along with social anthropology and the history of education. We make judgmental decisions which are not predictive of outcomes, and although theories based on a study of actual events, such as theories of learning, are available, the fact that they exist in such variety testifies to the paucity of our understanding of these processes. But we can turn to the work of philosophers with more confidence and base a curriculum design on a view of education. And in developing the design in practice, we will respond as teachers, both singly and in groups, in a variety of sophisticated ways to the internal and external constraints of the individual school and its community. It is more of an art than a science, and the good engineer has always thought of his activities in those terms too. Each new design, whether of a bridge or a chemical plant, is constrained by local conditions. His general view of the design will reflect publicly accepted norms linking art and function, and in its practical execution he will make use of data descriptive of previous experience with regard to the kind of structure or the expected chemical reactions. These data will, in a predictive sense, be more dependable than those offered by learning theories; but the fact that bridges collapse and that plants fail to come on stream as desired shows that the data cannot take the engineer all the way. His professional judgment will depend on common sense, practical experience and imagination.

This is not to suggest that education and curriculum are congruent with engineering. We are concerned with a different field with its own distinct principles and procedures. But it does, I think, suggest that if we look, as we are trying to, at the teacher in a school which is a focus for curriculum development, then the way he works has much more in common with the art and adaptability of the engineer than the convergent skills of the scientist or the deductive certainties of the academic researcher. There is much research to do, and its contribution is essential; but the theoretic mode must be kept in perspective. At present it is hard to avoid the conclusion that it has become dominant, and this is obstructing our understanding of curriculum implementation.

Second, let us compare the description above of the innovating teacher at work with a description Richard Rodgers (1976) gives of his feelings as a young musical-comedy composer:

> It was my first chance to examine the relationship between writing and audience reaction, to learn that what appears to be one thing on paper often undergoes a mysterious change in performance. This, I later realised, is really the answer to the question we are continually asked in the theatre: 'How could such a smart man produce anything as bad as that?' The answer is that he simply does not know what he has until a live audience tells him. It is not a question of guessing: the producer, writers and composer all try to know in advance what the end result will be. . . .

There is undoubtedly a sense in which the innovating teacher is both creative artist and performer. He is not guessing when he devises curriculum materials; and without enjoying a feeling of creating something, he wouldn't bother to devise them anyway. And the element of performance not only shows up their inadequacies, but gives him the impetus either to re-write the whole number or change the story line.

Again, I must emphasise that the parallel can be taken too far. The teacher's view is not congruent with that of the actor or the composer. But he is collaborating in a creative enterprise, building on his experience and technique and he performs not once nightly but for four or five hours daily. It seems to me that these creative action aspects of the teacher's role have been seriously overlooked; perhaps because they are much more apparent when he is involved in all-too-rare styles of school-based curriculum development.

If the creative-action model is a valid description of these processes, there are important implications for both pre-service and in-service training. As Hoyle remarks (1975): 'Curriculum innovation requires change in the internal organisation of the school. Change in the internal organisation is a major innovation.' Discussing these implications is outside my present scope. But Hoyle's discussion in another paper (1970) of the role of the change agent in curriculum development has an important bearing on school-focused development and deserves attention. Reviewing strategies of planned organisational change in education, Hoyle considers the ways 'in which the head can create a receptiveness to innovation by his staff', and concludes that 'the crucial decision by the head and his staff would be to invite the collaboration of a change agent who would be the captive of neither the head nor his staff, but would interact with both . . .'. The role of the change agent goes much further than that of the national or local adviser, chiefly because it implies a much more exclusive association with a particular school and a particular curriculum strategy. Shipman (1974), however, gives an interesting and encouraging account of the work of the coordinators on the Keele Integrated Studies Project. He writes of 'the overwhelming approval of the work of the coordinators by the teachers in the schools' and says that 'these seconded teachers rapidly adapted to the role of curriculum developers and change agents'. Shipman adds that: 'Few of the insights in this book are original or traceable to the sociological approach used. They come primarily from the perception of the project team as it faced new problems and reported its experiences.' This bears out my view that curriculum insights in school-based development will owe much to an exploitation of the arts of the practical. Shipman comments also on the sad fact that, in spite of their success as change agents, the coordinators were unable to use the new skills they had acquired when the project ended; they reverted to their old jobs. As he says, 'there is no career structure in research and development within education.'

It seems essential that a renewed emphasis must be given to in-service education if schools are to be able to develop new and more effective curriculum designs, and if effective curriculum dissemination is to proceed. And while there is a role for courses and conferences separate from the school, the focus of this new emphasis must be the school itself. The LEA must recognise the nature of curriculum development tasks in schools, both in staffing allocations and extra grants, but also in more imaginative ways. For example, the residential staff conference in an LEA centre is a most valuable way of promoting and agreeing innovation strategies, and the cost of such an exercise – which is taking place, after all, in teachers' own time – should be completely met from LEA funds. At Sheredes School such a conference has become an annual event, and the conferences held to agree the fourth- and fifth-year curriculum, and decide on the programme for the sixth form, were absolutely vital to form the consensus support upon which these developments rested. But in every case a part of the cost has been met from school funds, which I was fortunately able to use in this way.

Even more important, though, to these new in-service education approaches will be a recognition of the vital role of the change agent. Both HMIs and LEA advisers will come to recognise, as they extend their perceptions of the way teachers work in innovating schools, that the kind of role performed by the coordinators in the Keele project cannot long remain absent from the permanent curriculum scene. Such a change-agent or consultant will, in Hoyle's analysis, have a direct relationship with the change process, and collaborate with staff in 'identifying problems, evolving solutions and achieving change'. The Keele example points, too, to the advantages of independence, for the coordinators were not on the staff of the school, nor employed by an agency like the LEA or DES with a power-coercive function, however attenuated. Their allegiance was to the project, that is, to the process of change in some established way. The independent consultant, paid by the LEA but hired in just the same way to promote change along mutually agreed lines, will offer just the same advantages and could prove an invaluable aid to school-based curriculum development.

Chapter 6

The Timetable as an Enabling Device

There can be few aspects of the secondary school to which so much of a mystique has become attached than that of constructing the timetable. I know of a school where the deputy head is proud to explain that the process begins immediately after Christmas, to ensure that all is ready for unveiling in July for use in the following September. And given the complexity of the task this school has wished on itself, his pride may be well founded. One hears too, of schools where the timetabling team overrun into the summer holidays, and just manage to produce the fruits of their martyrdom by the start of the new school year. There are certainly few schools where the business of timetabling is not seen as something altogether rather special, requiring arcane talents that would put a Babylonian priest to shame, and where the staff are almost disappointed if the timetabler does not exercise the privileges of a prima donna.

This is a state of affairs which does schools no credit whatever. Instead of seeing the timetable as a mechanism for extending the variety of learning strategies, it has become a straitjacket into which a narrowly conceived range of activities must fit or go to the wall. And in any case, the idea that months of planning are required each year in order that an organisation can determine its activities for the following year is one that could scarcely have been tolerated in a Victorian family business; let alone a sophisticated organisation in which a swift and sensitive response to changing conditions of finance and staffing will be a prerequisite if the best use is to be made of resources.

We can make other objections. Since the timetable will

determine the whole life of the school for a year, writing it needs to be made an accessible, not a reclusive business. It will not be possible to achieve everything that is desired; but there will always be a number of different ways of resolving a difficulty, and if the timetabling process is more accessible, the staff concerned can be consulted and can accept with a good grace the course of action finally chosen. And not to give each teacher, by the end of the summer term, the programme he will be following in the ensuing school year is not just discourteous; it means his planning for the new term must be based on guesswork rather than an accurate schedule, and this is simply unprofessional. But what is most disturbing about this whole approach to timetabling is that it is completely unnecessary.

The comprehensive school timetable has reached this absurd point because of a failure to think hard enough about the school's purpose. Nowhere does the attempt, in the curriculum of the first-generation comprehensive, to reconcile the two conflicting patterns of the grammar and of the modern school become exposed so clearly as in the difficulties it creates for the timetable. Because the grammar-school curriculum is exclusively subject based, there is a pressure in one direction to write the timetable exclusively as separate subject periods, and with ability setting in several subjects. But upon this tradition is superimposed the modern school emphasis on the child pursuing his own interests, and we have seen in Chapter 2 how this has given weight to the idea of the comprehensive school as a differentiating institution offering a variety of courses and subject options. Furthermore, the modern school has become associated in many teacher's minds with topic-based approaches, leading to countervailing pressures for 'integrated work', without any systematic curriculum planning to determine what this should be about, and what the underlying educational implications may be.

The result is that the timetable for the first five years will have to accommodate some or all of a number of elements which set up conflicting logistic pressures. Against the need for separate subject periods will be set a provision for perhaps a humanities operation, linking history and geography and RE say, in the first two years; then in the third year, the languages staff's insistence on a separate set for the second foreign language will require the introduction of a streamed organisation, even if this has not already been adopted in the first and second years; and finally, the needs of the differentiating comprehensive will be met by a fourth- and fifth-year curriculum which keeps about 20 per cent of the timetable in subject blocks, but distributes the rest between four to seven option columns, each containing enough subjects to absorb the whole year group on a choice basis. In practice, as I have pointed out, these option schemes have a streaming effect; but in many schools the streaming is explicit by arranging two kinds of option system in the fourth and fifth years, and offering a 'guided choice' between in effect two different education systems. The additional timetable complication is then that the 'academic' part will be subject options, but the 'non-academic' part will usually involve blocked time for integrated work with titles like 'Learning to Live', along with half- or sometimes whole-day sessions at the nearby college of further education for 'interest-based' vocational courses.

It is enough of a nightmare to set such a scheme out on paper, because its illogicality is both disturbing and wasteful. But that is a mere bagatelle compared with the problems of translating such a scheme into an arrangement of teachers and pupils into parcels that may vary in size from one teacher for 12 pupils, to six teachers for 180 pupils; and in time units that will vary from one-eighth of the day to half the day. Then there will be further constraints stemming possibly from the availability of teaching spaces, or from the externally imposed schedules of the college. Little wonder that there is never any time to sit down and think about re-planning the curriculum! And this is to leave out of consideration the sixth form, where there may well be yet another option scheme involving three or four columns for choosing A-level subjects, with other columns for O-levels and general studies courses. The difficulty with all subjects options is that they seek to bring together the very teachers whom the separate subjects in the lower school timetable keep apart. There are, indeed, former grammar schools where the importance of exernal validation takes the shape of writing the sixth-form timetable before that of the first five years; a clear sign of where the priorities are considered to lie.

Fortunately we can leave this chaotic system behind and see how the timetable can be not a constricting but an enabling device. Before we do so, though, it is worth mentioning two developments which such systems have brought into being as aids to the timetabling process. One is the idea of computer-assisted timetabling, which has replaced the earlier but in practice unrealisable dream of programming a computer to produce the entire timetable. For although the basic task of timetabling is easily understood, and each individual operation of completing a square is easy to execute, there are two problems in translating the process to a computer. First, a very considerable amount of information must be fed into the computer, and in such a form that the computer can understand it. Not only the desired allocation of teachers to pupils, but all the constraints which, if not observed, will make the result worthless. Second, the subsequent computing operation takes quite a lot of computer time, and is therefore not cheap. Then there is the fact that whereas 90 per cent, say, of a timetable can be done by hand quite quickly, making the remaining 10 per cent come out right, at least cost to the school's organisation and staff, is much the harder part. If this is to be done by computer, it means programming into the computer details of what final possible artifices may be used in order to effect a solution: that Miss Bloggsworthy, for example, will be prepared to teach up to four periods of remedial English providing she can still take the first year for science. That kind of information may lie in the brain of a deputy head, but it is a different matter to put it altogether onto punched cards.

The aficionados of computer timetabling have therefore accepted that in spite of all the work involved in preparing the input data, the result will in any case have to be completed by hand. Unless, that is, the timetable is for such a limited or straightforward organisation that it could be easily completed by hand in the first place. It seems hardly likely, therefore, that computer timetabling has much of a future; and so far it has hardly had a past.

The other development has been the devising of systems of curriculum notation and analysis. That of Davies (1969) has since become the basis of a DES system which has been hawked around fairly extensively by HMIs in recent years.

It is in essence simply a way of summarising the provision a school is making on its curriculum; the pattern of subjects, and also how the teaching staff are allocated to the separate subjects in each year of the school. This is convenient for national and local inspectors who are frequently interested in making comparisons between schools and authorities. Bald staffing ratios can be very misleading ; a simple notation system makes it possible to go beyond them and see how one school may work its teachers harder than another by giving them less free time, and also whether a school is underwriting a particularly lavish option scheme in the fourth and fifth years at the expense of large classes in the first three years – a not uncommon phenomenon. There are plainly advantages in putting such an analysis tool in the hands of senior staff, so that they can find out exactly what is happening.

But it is doubtful if anyone would have bothered to invent such systems were it not for the complications that the curriculum of the differentiating-style comprehensive school has given rise to. Of course it helps to know exactly into what pockets the school's limited resources are disappearing; but it is really an admission of failure that it needs a system of curriculum notation to find out. However, given the realities of present timetables, such a system will have some value in this narrow sense. And it is true that it can be used to cost proposed variations quickly. But it is hard not to avoid the conclusion that it is more likely to promote tinkering with the curriculum than an examination of basic questions. There is a sense, indeed, in which it diverts attention away from the real area of judgment, to more superficial questions about the effect of increasing options, extending remedial provision, enlarging forms and so on. For in truth, the basic arithmetic of such calculations is remarkably simple and will fit onto the back of most deputy-heads' envelopes. When all is said and done, notational analysis is a tool of very limited value.

Let us now look at an attempt to develop a timetabling approach which breaks away from the patterns we have so far discussed. It has been recognised for some time that the amount of work in timetabling would be reduced if it were possible to reduce the number of entries. For a start, if the number of weekly periods is reduced by increasing their length, then the task of timetabling must shrink proportionately. The 80-period, 10-day timetable must represent the worst of all possible worlds; and the 20-period, 5-day timetable probably the best. And it must be borne in mind that reducing complexity also increases accessibility; it is just simply easier to understand what is going on.

Further gains can be made if, instead of timetabling single subject periods, a number of subjects is grouped together and treated as a block. Then instead of, say, English for class 1A on Tuesday period 3, along with French for 1B and maths for 1C in the half-year group, the timetabler writes in 'humanities' for the whole period, and the initials of the teachers of English, geography and history. This is known as block timetabling, and it is then a matter for the head of humanities to decide how the half-year is to be timetabled as an internal task. In this example, the blocked subjects happen to make curriculum sense, or rather, they are capable, if properly planned, of making sense. But there is no reason why disparate subjects should not be blocked out in chunks in this way, if it can be justified.

It is clear that the weakness of blocking out, say, French, maths and drama together is that having done it, the problem of allocating space between these three dissimilar subjects is one that people will not rush to tackle. In the nature of things, therefore, the logic of block timetabling is that one brings together subjects which have enough in common to make the subsequent sub-timetabling reasonably convenient. With this proviso, the way is clear to bring the whole business of writing the timetable within a much smaller compass. And if blocking can be combined with fewer periods, then at a stroke the task takes on perfectly manageable proportions. One is left wondering why any school bothers with any other kind of timetable.

The reason is that blocking has important implications for curriculum and organisation. The most trivial – yet I have had it put to me – is that in some schools the head would not sanction the delegating of the sub-timetable to the heads of the subject blocks. But there are other more important objections. There is, for instance, little point in running just one block, for humanities; it will be necessary to contrive other blocks where the bedfellows may not be so willing. And if the first year is blocked, why not the second? What will happen in years 4 and 5, when blocking will come into conflict with options? Furthermore, blocking does not march easily with streaming. How can three ability-sets for English be formed in a half-year block for English, geography and history, with one teacher for each subject? It is difficult, too, to offer a second language on a selective basis in the second or third year without disruption to blocking patterns.

These are powerful objections in a school which is established on conventional lines. And it is right that the timetable, like examinations, should be determined by the curriculum rather than the other way round. It follows that block timetabling will be unattainable in most schools without either ingenious compromise or far-reaching changes in the school's underlying philosophy. To push block timetabling for its own sake is a bit like trying to sell gas fires to houses with only mains electricity, and may get the same uncomprehending response. It is a matter of a fundamental conversion.

But it is possible to introduce elements of blocking into the conventional timetable, and in some schools enthusiasm for blocking has been taken so far that the timetable has become, perversely, once again a determinant of the curriculum rather than its creature. For if we think of the timetable not in its educational context as a representation of teaching periods, but rather as an arrangement of symbols so permuted that the same two do not appear in the same column, then writing the timetable becomes a mathematical rather than an educational exercise. It is necessary to keep the number of symbols fairly small, to correspond to the number of different subject blocks, and also each block must occupy nearly the same amount of time on the timetable. And options must then lie either within the blocks, or be formed by combinations of blocks.

Such an approach, which has been termed consistent blocking, certainly solves the problem of timetabling, because the timetable is then merely a grid of symbols which can represent a fleet of lorries or an assembly line just as well as a set of classrooms. The act of writing the timetable is simply that of transcribing the symbols into the appropriate educational language. But in effect the wheel has come full circle. Just as the traditional timetable inhibits change because it is so complicated, here we have a timetable which constricts the curriculum because it is so simple. For it is by no means easy to ensure that the blocks of subjects which make up the timetable are of nearly the same size, without making up blocks which raise fundamental curriculum issues. For example, a block of humanities subjects is bound to be an obvious choice, and will take up 4 to 5 70-minute periods weekly if it includes 2 or 3 subjects. Mathematics, on the other hand, may well be only 2 periods weekly in some years in the school; and this will be so for science. But the solution of combining mathematics and science into one faculty block is neat logistically rather than philosophically. And the condition that requires options to be formed between blocks is likely to constrain difficult choice areas like the fourth and fifth year, where the option scheme must allow genuine provision for choice of personal skills and career subjects. Consistent blocking, in short, takes tidiness a bit too far for curriculum comfort.

We can, however, see that the combination of block timetabling and fewer periods is as attractive as ever. But in order to be able to use it, it implies a curriculum which is not subject-based; is non-streamed; makes educational sense of a faculty structure; and which sustains such a structure over all five years, with a minimal use of options. But these, of course, are exactly the attributes of the common culture curriculum which has been described in previous chapters. And block timetabling into fewer periods means faculty timetabling into the longer periods we need in order to develop a sufficient variety of learning strategies. Furthermore, the requirement that each subject-block allocates its own sub-timetable is a virtue; for it means that the faculty head then can extend his autonomy into the most effective arrangement of staff teams within the available space. And, of course, the concept of the common curriculum naturally ensures that the first five years are seen in faculty terms as an educational continuum.

There is, then, a further sense in which the common curriculum, as advanced here, is *sui generis* the structure for the comprehensive school; for the ideal form of timetable to enable it to be effected is precisely the form which is most readily mastered and most easily understood. Our task must now be to see how the common curriculum can be converted into a block timetable so as to give the fullest opportunity for staff involvement and the most effective expresssion, as individual timetables for staff and pupils, of the ideal it represents.

The first step will be to invite heads of faculties to submit lists of their preferred allocation of staff to each of the year teams. They will take into account both staff specialisms and staff involvement in preliminary planning, as well as important requirements external to curriculum considerations; for example, that the first-year tutor should be a member of the first-year humanities team, or the need, because of shortage of space, to block out say the second- and fourth-year humanities teams into the same timetable slots, and hence to give each team different personnel. This process will also take account of any likely expansion or contraction in the school, and will therefore have implications for staffing in general. It is likely that heads of faculty will begin general discussions of the various possibilities in separate talks with the head during the autumn term, even though the final decisions will rest on the outcome of LEA budget wrangles and not be known until the following February or even later. The link between staffing and curriculum planning is so intimate that it is difficult to penetrate the logic of a head delegating the latter task to a director of curriculum studies. And by the same token, the timetable is so exclusively the expression of the curriculum that the head will be wise who maintains a close personal involvement with the process of writing it. This, of course, is made easier by the simpler layout of the block timetable.

The next step need not be taken until May. By this time any additional appointments will, with luck, have been made and the only uncertainty will be the replacement of existing staff who give notice at the end of that month. The head will have a fair idea of what can be expected from this quarter, and so it makes sense to take a large sheet of paper and set out on it who will be teaching what. This schedule can then be agreed with heads of faculty and any other staff who are concerned, and finally made the basis of the putative timetable at the beginning of June. The rows on the schedule will represent the years of pupils, including the sixth, and the columns will be headed with the faculties, option columns and a space for remedial allocations. The year teams can then be written in for each faculty, and staff allocated to option subjects. Sixth-form subjects can be written in, for the sake of convenience, under whichever faculty headings seem appropriate; the object of the schedule is simply to distribute staffing among all the perceived teaching commitments of the school. If the thinking during the previous six months has gone smoothly, there will be no unpleasant surprises disclosed by the schedule; but there will always be minor adjustments to ensure that the teaching loads of individual staff match their responsibilities, and to allow for any imposed change in part-time staffing. At this stage general part-time dispositions can be made, but only on a provisional basis since these can provide useful flexibility in the timetabling process.

The question of teaching loads needs careful thought. In a week of 20 periods each of 70 minutes, the normal unadjusted load is unlikely to be less than 16 periods or more than 18. But with a staff of 50 or 60, it is clear that the difference between these figures represents over a hundred teacher periods. This is a question of curriculum policy rather than timetabling, but it is convenient to discuss it in connection with timetabling since it is always at this stage in planning that it becomes prominent. At first sight, the temptation is to select the higher figure, with its suggestion of increased productivity and therefore smaller classes or perhaps more options. And it may be that staffing cuts leave little choice in the matter; either loads are increased, or the timetabled provision is reduced.

But increasing the basic load does not produce something for nothing. Not only will the teacher in an innovating school be involved, outside the classroom, in all the usual extra-curricular activities, and in correction and preparation; he will bear the additional burden of taking part in a creative process. This means even more time devoted to planning meetings, and also a more imaginative, many-sided role in the classroom than in a school with a static concept of curriculum. It may be true, of course, that smaller classes, and therefore higher loads, will ease the teaching burden; and certainly a class size in the 25 to 30 range will be the maximum for non-streamed work. But it is clear that to see teacher productivity simply in terms of class contact hours is not only to go for quantity at the expense of teaching quality;

it may make all the difference between a staff enjoying a stimulating commitment to school-based curriculum development, and one where everyone is simply too tired to think of anything fresh. There are no management analyses and nomograms to give quantitative answers to decisions of this kind; schools are about people rather than neat little diagrams. This is why informal modes of communication are so necessary in the innovating school; it is the spoken, not the written word which tells of a teacher's feelings, his understanding, his involvement with his pupils and his colleagues. The deputy head who sees his task as the movement of pieces of paper from one tray into another will know nothing of this. But it is for the head to allocate roles; and to make one deputy responsible for curriculum implementation will at once take him out of his chair and on to his feet, and lead him to talk to staff rather than write notes to them.

Similar questions arise in considering what adjustments are to be made to the basic load in recognition of additional responsibilities. It seems reasonable that a head of faculty should not teach more than 15 periods, in general; but academic responsibility is as a rule well rewarded by additional salary payments and this needs to be taken into account. It is also true that most of the extra work it involves can be done out of class time. But with pastoral posts pupils need to be seen during school time as a rule, and it can happen that the need to attract well-qualified staff to academic posts leaves less extra money for staff with demanding pastoral roles. These are factors for consideration by the individual school. But it is reasonable to allow a deduction of at least 2 periods from the basic load for a year tutor, and adjustments will also be needed to take into account tasks like counselling, exam administration and so on. Ultimately these must be seen as matters for negotiation with the head, because they involve a delicate balance between salary, the intensive or extensive nature of the task, and other responsibilities or expectations like school productions.

All this will be known and established and incorporated on the pre-timetabling schedule. But it will also be understood that the schedule represents an ideal state. For example, the English department may have arranged their representation in the teams for humanities and expressive arts so as to obtain a desirable degree of overlap between the two faculties; and the modern languages department may have staffed the second-year team so as to provide continuity with that of the present first-year team. But everyone knows that the timetable will be a compromise. The constraints on it are such that universal perfection is impossible. The aim must be to produce a timetable which is the fairest attainable solution. It is therefore very desirable that, at this stage, heads of faculties should indicate an order of priority in their requirements, and also what concessions they are prepared to make in order to achieve a particular end. Thus the head of science might state that he is so keen to see a team of four, rather than the usual three, staff for each half-year in the fourth and fifth years that he is prepared to accept some degree of substitution of personnel in the teams for the second and third year. Without conditional statements of this kind, it would not be possible to get an optimum timetable solution. Yet it is statements of precisely this kind which do not lend themselves to expression as a computer input. The timetable is nothing if it is not a human document.

All is now set for timetabling proper to begin. This can be done with pieces of paper on a cardboard sheet, with names of staff pencilled onto the paper. But colour coding the faculties and options helps, and it is an advantage to be able to move the layout around from room to room. It is possible to buy, in shops selling business equipment, metal sheets coated with a white plastic enamel and ruled up in a number of grid patterns. These are used with flexible coloured plastic shapes which adhere magnetically to the sheet, but can be peeled off and replaced at will. They are intended for business planning, but are ideal for faculty timetabling since all the information can be expressed in a small compass. They also have the advantage of cheapness. One chooses a metal sheet or sheets ruled in the most convenient way, and marks it out using adhesive white paper tape which is also available. This may also be easily removed to make changes. And the different staff are represented by small adhesive coloured plastic shapes, which adhere to the flexible faculty pieces but can be peeled away if the personnel in a team changes. These shapes are no more than 5 mm square, and offer sufficient variety for well over 100 staff. They are so cheap they can be regarded as disposable. Flexible pieces will be needed in two sizes: one to represent a half-year group, about 15 mm x 30 mm (so that one of these above the other is a whole year group); and another about 15 mm x 5 mm, to represent a period with a single teaching group. The latter will be necessary only for the sixth-form. Both are available in enough colours to allow easy distinction between faculties and option columns. In this way the timetable for a six-form entry 11–18 school can be worked out and displayed on two sheets with a total area of about 600 mm x 800 mm.

The act of timetabling has become associated in the popular mind with mathematical skills, but I have noticed all staff, regardless of specialism, are able to make shrewd contributions when shown a layout of the type described. Care and concentration are all that are needed. The only fundamental rule is to start with the most difficult entries, and finish with the easiest. For a timetable is the reverse of a jigsaw, which gets easier as it proceeds. In timetabling, one starts off with all options open, and steadily forfeits them as the spaces are filled. It is therefore essential that the first entries are those which will tolerate scarcely any change, since if these were left to the end of the operation an impossible position would soon result. The same rule must apply at every stage; if there are more constraints on mathematics than on expressive arts, then mathematics takes priority. These decisions are not always obvious, and it is far more important that the timetabler have an intimate knowledge of both the school buildings, the curriculum structure and the teaching personnel than a degree in mathematics. He will also need the capacity to make narrowly balanced judgments. It seems likely that the head or a deputy will be best suited to this task.

The order of entry will therefore be peculiar to each school, and indeed may change from year to year. Humanities may well go in first, since it is the largest faculty in terms of teaching time, and also runs across whole-year groups. Creative activities might go in next, and at this stage it will be necessary to insert any sixth-form periods which involve a team of 4 or more staff; for example, the three central studies periods discussed in Chapter 8. Otherwise it will be impossible to draw together teams which involve representatives from several faculties. By now the option periods in years 4 and 5 must be inserted, and if these involve a contribution from another institution like a college of further education, it may be necessary to give them top priority. It is likely that the remaining entries can be made in the order: science, mathematics, languages and expressive arts. The wise timetabler will work out in advance the amount of space each faculty takes up, and the degree of flexibility in staffing each of them. This will be the best guide to the final order. It is also important in these closing stages to insert games periods at times which make sense; plainly the last period of the day is better than the first. There is more flexibility on PE periods, which can be invaluable in the final moves.

Throughout, the greatest attention must be paid to the rhythm of the timetable for each half-year group of pupils. It is not just a matter of avoiding obvious nonsenses, like consecutive games and PE, or two mathematics periods on the same day; it is important to secure enough general variety in each day, and to keep an eye on the balance of the whole week. These are factors which sometimes have to go to the wall in conventional 40-period week timetables. In a 20-period faculty timetable, it is both possible and desirable to ensure that the four periods in each day make up a rounded programme.

As timetabling proceeds, heads of faculty and individual staff will be brought in and consulted on difficulties. Modified teams may be needed, with several possibilities; the best people to consult are those directly affected. Or perhaps a sought-after spread of mathematics periods through the fifth-year week can be achieved only by rearranging science lessons and thus imposing eight concurrent science classes at one time, instead of seven. But perhaps one of the classes can go into other accommodation; inter-faculty arrangements of this kind will make the best use of the school's facilities.

By the end of June, the whole timetable may well be complete. The last entries will be the sixth-form timetable, compiled not on the basis of option columns but *ad hoc*, from the actual combinations asked for by the incoming lower sixth, and incorporating those already established in the present lower sixth. Working from a list of which subjects can be timetabled together, each period is inserted in turn, taking teachers as available from the stock of spare teachers at the foot of the column for each period in the week. In this way, the constraint exercised by choice is kept to the actual minimum needed. The use of option columns, in contrast, will always introduce more choice than is needed, or indeed than is desirable. For even the simplest systems will allow some combinations which no careers teacher could support. The result is to introduce a degree of redundancy, in the language of information theory, into the problem. To cope with this extra constraint, something has to give. In a school with a really large sixth of 120 or more, the sixth form will attract a more favourable staffing from the LEA and this may give the extra flexibility needed to provide option columns. But in the small sixth, the extra constraint could be met only by breaking up faculty teams in the lower school. Given the small average size of comprehensive school sixth forms, there is every advantage in operating an *ad hoc* system.

With the timetable complete, two further benefits of a faculty-based common curriculum can now be enjoyed. First, there is no need to produce the corresponding rooms timetable. For the school will be divided into faculty areas, and pupils and staff will know where to go when humanities appears on the timetable. The head of faculty will allocate space as required. For option subjects, it is a simple matter for the timetabler to work out where there are spare rooms and make up a brief list. In the same way a simple reference chart can be completed showing the take-up of accommodation through the week.

The second benefit is the ease with which the timetable can be converted to printed form. The timetable for each year fits easily onto a single A4 sheet, with space for showing the homework timetable too. Each sheet can be cut lengthwise (see Appendix) to yield the timetable for a half-year group, and so each pupil can be given his timetable at minimum cost in the first period of the new school year. From the second period on, normal school can begin. And the timetable for the whole school will occupy only A4 typescript sheets. Each member of staff can be given his personal copy, showing the entire structure of the common curriculum, well before the summer term ends.

Chapter 7

Subjects and Options

In considering the detailed structure of a common culture curriculum in Chapters 3 and 4, we have seen that an approach based on an initiation of all pupils into forms of knowledge and understanding does not exclude the conceptual frameworks and teaching skills of existing school subjects. It is rather a matter of adapting and extending them in the light of the new curriculum strategy, with the paramount implication of new styles of implementation and management discussed in Chapter 5. But such an approach does make it possible to take a fresh look at the accretion of irrelevant data, topics and even subjects which the traditional view of the comprehensive school as a differentiating institution has allowed to clog up the curriculum. Another unfortunate effect has been to sharpen the distinction between educational and social needs, and to some extent sacrifice the former to the latter. The intimate connection between a pupil's social identity and his learning in a school has been brought out in Chapter 5, and I shall return to this in discussing pastoral care in Chapter 9.

I should like in this chapter to look a little more closely at some subjects whose curriculum treatment shows marked variation, and in particular at three which the DES has recently suggested are cause for some concern in comprehesive schools; modern languages, mathematics and science. The two latter are both components of our compulsory five-year core, and on any analysis of our culture they would seem certain to be regarded in that light. But that this is by no means so at present in schools is clear from a Schools Council Research Study (1973), on the examination courses of first-year sixth-formers:

> The fact that, if the main fifth form subjects have not been studied at O/CSE, they are rarely followed at A Level, emphasises the importance of subject decisions, many of them frequently made as far back as the third year (or its equivalent) of secondary school. Girls, in particular, decide not to continue studying any physical science at a very early stage in their school careers. By their choices at that time many young people are effectively closing the options available to them in the sixth form.

With science, the only effective way to avoid this is to prevent it from splitting into three separate subjects at fourth year level. For as the survey declared, 'it is questionable whether a balanced curriculum can be provided within an eight-subject framework at O level if more than two languages or more than two sciences are studied.' But with separate science subjects, physics is often the one that is dropped, and especially by girls.

With mathematics, the fear is that it will be quietly dropped from the fourth- and fifth-year curriculum not by potential sixth-formers, but by pupils who have become unresponsive to it, yet who will thus be denied a level of competence and a degree of insight into one of the most distinctive forms of understanding man has invented. Achieving this for all pupils is certainly a difficult task, but the cultural view suggests it must be attempted; while the instrumental view argues that mathematical skills are so useful to industry that the attempt must be made and must succeed.

Let us, though, consider modern languages first, which is in a very different position. There is no agreement that it should be compulsory as an O-level or CSE subject, either on cultural or instrumental grounds. And the nature and purpose of teaching a foreign language to this level are the subject of disagreement among modern linguists themselves. The debate is both active and often bitter, and by no means unimportant. The fervent espousal of primary French, for instance, has meant much outlay of cash and teachers' time, and also diverted resources from other forms of language teaching; yet, as the NFER report *Primary French in the Balance* (Burstall, 1974) has shown, the project was based on unverifiable premises about the optimum age for learning a foreign language, and has signally failed to improve the acquisition of language skills. As a secondary school subject, there is evidence that it is both unpopular (in 1970, Schools Council 'Enquiry One' ranked it with music and religious instruction as the least interesting subjects) and unsuccessful (in 1972, the NFER report by Ross *et al.* on comprehensive education showed the success rate for modern languages was the lowest compared with mathematics, science and English). We must therefore look closely at arguments for extending languages teaching, and at different views of how this could be done.

The assertion that every child should learn a language to a standard that will give him access to another nation's cultural heritage is one which reappears from time to time, and is usually offered without any supporting arguments, presumably on the assumption that it can be accepted as a self-evident truth. We have seen, though, that it is insupportable on a Hirstian view of liberal education, and the proposition is not a popular one with teachers of foreign languages, who know all too well how much time and effort is needed to reach a stumbling competence in many pupils, let alone a command of the tongue that will unlock the beauties of Racine or the grandeurs of Goethe. In fact, there is no defined syllabus for the language component of O- and A-level in any examination board's modern languages syllabus, neither as a rule are the lexis and syntax of grammar specified. This argument seems to rest on emotion rather than reason, and is usually propounded by public- or grammar-school heads to whom the notion that a gentleman must know a European language perhaps harks back nostalgicaly to the days of the Grand Tour.

The instrumental argument is, however, another matter, and since our entry into the EEC, it has become fashionable to talk of the needs of a trading nation, and to make unfavourable comparisons with the ease with which the Dutch (if not, perhaps, the French) learn two or three languages as well as their own. The suggestion is that, as good Europeans and exporters, compulsory education should aim at language competence in French or German for all. We can see at once that the language tasks of the school are being defined rather differently than when the cultural argument is the basis. Clarity about the aims of languages teaching is particularly important, as Hirst and Peters (1970) point out:

> Suppose . . . he is a teacher of French. Is his aim simply to enable his pupils to rub along all right during holidays in France? Does he hope that they will eventually be able to write French? Does he envisage the learning of the language as the best way of coming to understand, from the inside, the form of life of another nation? Or is his aim just the non-educational one of getting through an examination?

In practice, the aims of modern languages teachers vary greatly. Some consider verbal fluency in the language and life of the country concerned to be the only realistic aim; others regard the job as not worth doing if written skills and the structure of the language are not included. For some, the answer is to include the language as a component of a 'European studies' course; but these are often a non-linguistic sop offered in years 4 and 5 to pupils who have effectively failed in the study of a foreign language, and raise serious problems of curriculum aims and content which have been mentioned in Chapter 3. Others see such courses as anathema; the language is either worth learning as a language, or not at all. To jumble it up with history or geography is to throw away all it stands for.

At this stage, one or two facts are useful. For example, in the last ten years, the proportion of the 11–plus age group studying a foreign language has more than doubled; and numbers of first-year undergraduates taking languages courses are steady over the years 1971–3, with an increase in the number on four-year courses. And as for industry's need for linguists, a study at York University, reported by Hawkins (1976) reveals that 'employers have virtually no interests in linguists, a study at York University reported by Hawkins (1976) reveals that 'employers have virtually no interest in who have a language as well as marketable skills'. Looking at the sixth form and beyond, Hawkins adds that 'very few serious linguists will – if they are well advised – aim to make their career as linguists'.

Even if there were enough languages teachers available, it is difficult to support the argument that schools need to compel all pupils to take a foreign language for five years. The true needs of industry are both different, and more limited. Trying to hammer language skills into unwilling 15- and 16-year-olds is both wasteful and unsettling for staff and students alike. Motivation is always important to learning, and in many subjects skilful teaching and thoughtful curriculum design can engender it. But motivating an unwilling English child to learn French with the enthusiasm and intensity that give pace and understanding is simply impossible in the context of practical economics. It is far better to take a tip from the idea of *l'éducation permanente*, and set up skills centres for language learning, based in further and higher education institutions, where concentrated courses can be provided for willing learners. And meanwhile, in schools, effort should be concentrated on giving all secondary pupils a lively and intense course for the first three years, and on developing foreign language examinations at 16-plus which are geared to a searching study of the different kinds of aims and skills which languages teaching might adopt.

In mathematics teaching, the cardinal fact of life is that the response of each child to the range of mathematical activities is different. And children acquire an understanding of concepts and skills at different rates. It is true, too, as the SMP booklet on manipulative skills points out (School Mathematical Project, 1974), that 'mathematics is a subject in which, more often than not, things are either right or wrong . . . [but] society is disposed to place less insistence than it did a generation ago on personal qualities of precision, unfailing accuracy and attention to detail'. Given, therefore, the difficulties of introducing mathematics to all pupils in these times, we should be encouraged by this finding of a report from the Engineering Training Board (March 1977), which looked at school mathematics learning and the performance of young craft and technician trainees: 'Trainee engineers who have been taught modern mathematics at school perform better on training courses than those who learnt mathematics by traditional methods.' The report is based on a four-year research study, and lends support to the view – in spite of vocal if unsubstantiated opinions to the contrary – that modern mathematics is a curriculum innovation which has strengthened pupil engagement and understanding.

But few mathematics teachers would see the finding as grounds for complacency. There is still a long way to go. Too many pupils leave at 16 untouched by mathematical ideas, and within mathematics teaching there is little real agreement on what its aims and content should be, and how a really effective five-year course could operate for all pupils. Most schools have introduced modern maths topics into their courses to 16-plus exams, and this is paralleled by their appearance in mode 1 examinations from many boards, and in published texts. Reviewing a new series of books recently, however, Howson (1976) remarks:

> It is now almost 15 years since the major upheaval of the secondary school mathematics curriculum and it would be reasonable, therefore, to assume that the 'modern' contribution . . . would be those features of the new curricula that had most to offer to mathematical education . . . Rather it would seem to be the case that what has survived has been in the main that which can be easily taught, easily examined, and easily crammed.

It is likely that in many schools, notation like set language is taught as a definition, in the same arid way so familiar in the traditional approach, and not exploited at all as a mathematical device. Other schools may use SMP materials and take SMP or similar modern maths exams, but without introducing new teaching methods which allow genuine mathematical activity to flower. And in these schools, sixth-form pupils would go on to take a traditional course to A-level.

Where SMP has been adopted in a competent and thoroughgoing manner, it is generally recognised (as the project itself accepts) that the original course gave insufficient emphasis to manipulative skills and drills in algebra and basic numerical operations. To correct this is not a difficult matter and in any case, the basis for the learning programme will be not a hamper of materials but school-based curriculum development by the team of staff involved. This will include, as I have stressed in Chapter 4, a set of refined techniques to monitor the progress of each child in a systematic way. Such a department is unlikely to retain ability setting for mathematics in the first three years. Only a non-streamed format can do justice to the way individual children can move ahead when a learning block has been cleared away, and see the subject as one of opportunity rather than limitation. The result will be increased engagement and greater fulfilment. The teacher will spend his nervous energy not on sustaining attention, but on team-based curriculum planning.

The question still remains whether SMP can be a satisfactory basis for a five-year course for all. In her 1975 presidential address to the Mathematical Association, Hayman declared:

> Much later, SMP started to modify its courses for less able pupils, but they remain essentially academic. They are pursuing the myth that if you speak a foreign language sufficiently slowly, you will be understood; that the difficulties in the subject are due to the speed at which it is taught, rather than the nature of the mathematical concepts involved.

This view echoes, in extreme form, the feeling many convinced modern maths teachers have that SMP is an excellent course for the mathematically talented, and capable of effective extension to most of the ability range; but with substantial limitations at the lower-middle and bottom. Some feel, too, that the above-average but not outstanding pupils are not served as well by it as they would like. As long ago as 1968, Hammersley queried the 'I do, and I understand' emphasis of the SMP/Nuffield zealots:

> Is it necessary first to understand the underlying theory before learning how to utilize some mathematical technique? Far too much stress can be laid on learning a subject 'properly', according to the accepted canons of the day. A belief . . . that in mathematics you must proceed sequentially from the root to the branches . . . is didactically bad. There are many by-ways to understanding . . . It is often more important to find the right solution to a problem than to understand the logic of the method.

More recently, Malpas (1974) has examined the SMP books A to H, which are easily the most popular, and looked at the relationship between the practical illustration of a topic, and its treatment as an abstraction. He concludes:

> Many early chapters begin with experimental investigations with the object of abstracting mathematics from them but, from the fact that few refer back to the problems investigated at the beginning, it appears that it was the abstraction and not the situations which really interested the authors. Later chapters are applying mathematical skills to real problems, but very frequently skills established a long time before.

There will, in any case, always be a tension between those who see mathematics as a pure and very Greek private world for mathematicians to enjoy, and those who see it as a service industry, inventing tools for scientists and engineers to use and create wealth with. But fortunately, a great many mathematicians realise that this tension has a creative value, and works both ways; much new mathematics results from attempts to use mathematical methods to solve real-life problems. And although it is absurd to say that the only real mathematics is useless mathematics, what many scientists demand as 'useful maths' is merely petty manipulation. It is encouraging, though, to learn that the Centre for Science Education is developing inter-disciplinary materials on topics like ratios, rates and measurement. There is much to be gained by maths-science cooperation of this sort, and it can be particularly helpful to arrange an exchange of teachers between these departments. I have found that science staff, for example, enjoy teaching modern mathematics as part of their timetable, and their presence at maths department meetings can be refreshing.

My own view is that secondary school mathematics needs to pay much more attention to mathematical models, as abstract ways of describing real situations. This approach would at once not only relate mathematical abstraction to the world about us, but would also reveal its imaginative power to extend our understanding in ways which would be impossible without it. It would not, however, be a matter of revamping existing courses; it would need a fundamentally fresh approach. It is easy to take topics like sets, number bases, symmetries and transformations out of context from the present SMP course, and treat them as a bag of tricks rather than mathematical language, because the SMP course has not succeeded in embedding them as vital elements in a mathematical narrative. This is partly because it is essentially a first-generation course; and partly because it is perhaps biased away from the modelling approach of the applied mathematician towards that of the pure theoretician. Instead of making reality peripheral to central abstractions, there is everything to be gained from centrally exploiting real applications, and developing the abstractions outwards from them. In this way school mathematics could link more closely with other faculties; science of course, but also with geography, music, art and handicraft. There would also be scope for schools to derive material from local industry. Devices like pocket calculators should be welcomed as opening the door not only to the use of realistic data for mathematical models and calculations of hire purchase, mortgages and so on, but also to numerical solutions of equations, investigation of sequences and limits, and generally as a way of easing aside computation and letting the mathematics shine through. The scope of such a course would fit perfectly the aims of a common culture curriculum.

Turning now to science in the comprehensive school, there would seem to be a number of arguments for looking afresh at the variety of existing projects, in the light both of the need to avoid premature specialisation, and to relate science education to the concept of the common curriculum. Nowhere is the haphazard pattern of British curriculum development more vividly apparent than in secondary science, where six projects overlap in the five years of compulsory schooling.

In years 1 and 2, there is a straight choice between three projects which each aim at the whole ability range. The best established is Nuffield Combined Science, which was seen as 'an attempt to recapture the unity of outlook and consistency of method which belongs to the whole of science'. It amounts to ten pupils' booklets and three teachers' guides, covering ten subject areas like Looking for Patterns; How Living Things Begin; Air; Energy. The aim has been 'to produce a source of ideas, materials and comment to allow teachers to devise their own courses'. There is much scope for teacher initiative, and for practical work; but also considerable emphasis on content and factual recall. Scottish Integrated Science has some penetration south of the border, and is more structured than Combined Science, and more suitable for pupils going on to O-level. And Science 5/13 is based on behavioural objectives, with the aim of 'developing an enquiring mind and a scientific approach to problems'. The topics have titles like Time, Science from Toys, Change; apparatus is simple, and the basis is a project approach which, in middle schools, can be linked with other curriculum areas. Its adoption in junior schools would seem to be slight, which is unfortunate; and there is little penetration into secondary schools. The aims are mainly in the process area, with some emphasis on concepts. The project basis does not lend itself to the specialist structure of most secondary schools.

In years 3, 4 and 5, there is no single project aimed at the whole ability range. Nuffield Secondary Science is intended for those 'who are unlikely to take O-level in science', and is based on the proposal that such a course should have 'significance for the pupils' (Schools Council Working Paper 1). It is an assembly of detailed material ignoring traditional science subject boundaries, arranged under eight themes through which the teacher steers a route: Continuity of Life, Harnessing Energy, Movement, and so on. It is strong on human biology, uses worksheets and circuses extensively, and needs much laboratory preparation. Only parts of it are suitable for pupils below the reach of a conventional CSE.

For abler pupils, the choice is between separate Nuffield courses in physics, chemistry and biology, or the integrated approach of the Schools Council Integrated Science Project (SCISP). Many teachers regard the fully fledged Nuffield approach as suitable only for the most able. A number of schools use the approach and experiments as a part of orthodox courses. SCISP is based on behavioural objectives derived from Bloom and Gagné, aiming at 'a unified study rather than an increasingly artificial separation into separate uncoordinated disciplines'. It offers a two O-level certification requiring only 20 per cent of curriculum time, and the third-year course is devised 'in such a way that it can lead sensibly to work in either CSE or O-level during the fourth and fifth years'. Four pupils' books deal with themes like Building

Blocks, Interaction, Energy and Change. Social issues are discussed, and there is plenty of scope for teacher initiative in planning the individual school's course.

The evolution of the Nuffield courses has been discussed by MacDonald and Walker (1976). There are strong parallels with similar developments at the time in American science education: 'Both, more or less independently, arrived at versions of an objectives model and worked to a design that formed a prototype for Havelock's Research, Development and Diffusion model.' But each of the Nuffield teams had its own variation:

> The chemists worked their way intuitively towards something closely resembling Bloom's taxonomy of objectives and talked about 'education through chemistry'. The physicists stressed the phrase 'science for understanding'. The biologists struggled to bring experimental methods into a field dominated by description.

Reflecting on the adoption of the projects in schools, however, Becher (1971) has written: 'Far from "getting the message" implicit in the work of the development team, many teachers have superimposed their own very different interpretations and philosophies.' Without a doubt, the Nuffield courses have had a remarkable and energising effect on secondary school science. Huge sums of money were found for new equipment, and developments like SCISP have been possible only because of the Nuffield intervention, which could only have been done through a separate subject approach. But the expected reinstatement of science as a popular subject has not come about, and it may be that a continuing emphasis by science teachers on expository rather than heuristic teaching styles has something to do with it (Hornsby-Smith, 1975). There is some similarity here between Nuffield science and SMP maths: both generated a change of content, but without the looked-for accompanying reform in method.

In retrospect, the development of SCISP looks like a far-sighted Schools Council initiative in 1969. There was not the undercurrent of pressure towards integration to compare with that from the Association for Science Education that sparked off the Nuffield reform in the early 1960s, and it is therefore perhaps not surprising that it has so far made no marked impact in secondary schools. For one thing, there is the traditional conservatism of science teachers towards their separate specialisms, which the Nuffield courses have, ironically, reinforced; but much more important I think is that the case for integrated science looks really powerful only in the context of coherent curriculum planning, and of the common curriculum in particular. It is true that the evidence quoted at the beginning of this chapter puts the blame for premature specialisation squarely on three-subject science schemes in fourth-year option choice, and this points plainly towards an integrated two-subject course. But premature specialisation has long been an objectionable feature of the English grammar school, and it needs a major curriculum depth-charge to give the shake-up that will lead to total re-planning rather than piecemeal compromise.

There are also, of course, arguments which see science as part of our culture, and therefore as an integrated experience. The 1961 policy statement of the Science Masters' Association came quite close to this, with its emphasis on coherence:

> Science should be recognised – and taught – as a major human activity which explores the realm of human experience, maps it methodically but also imaginatively, and by disciplined speculation, creates a coherent system of knowledge.

The absence, too, of any instrumental arguments should be noted. To suggest that science is taught because industry needs it is to take a narrow view that could seriously distort school courses. The view of integration taken by SCISP seems to be centred on the three concepts of energy, building blocks and interaction, rather than a more penetrating attempt to look at the nature of scientific knowledge and how it could be given coherence in a school course. The introduction of some social science seems, for example, peripheral to integrated science itself. The project team might usefully have included a philosopher to consider these matters. The fact that 'energy' is a fundamental idea which gives a theoretical unity to the concept of integration that the other two do not possess has been pointed out by Pring (1975): 'what is open to criticism is the inadequate logical analysis of the interdisciplinary relationship between the respective disciplines. A theoretical unity is claimed that, in many respects, is not there.' The notion of integration is such a slippery one that it is bound to attract philosophical attention. But it seems likely that logical questions of this type have never been to the fore in any of the courses summarised above. The statements of aims seem to depend more on rhetoric than curriculum analysis; the objectives on some convenient psychological theory; and the materials on the pragmatic enthusiasm of teacher teams, much as for SMP. One can, however, do much worse than this, as a look at some of the American SMSG maths texts will show.

But one can also, surely, do much better. The time is ripe for an appraisal of science education projects, with the particular task of preparing the ground for a coherent, five-year integrated course that will make use largely of existing apparatus, but from the beginning be conceived for the whole ability range as leading to a single-subject integrated science examination or certificate, and offering additional material to provide a second subject for those pupils opting in the fourth and fifth year for extra science. Planning for the basic course should be much more searching than hitherto with regard to the philosophy of science and interrelationships between the separate subjects. Popper's view that 'The method of science is the method of bold conjectures and ingenious and severe attempts to refute them' should be more in evidence both in prior planning and in organising the learning. A decade's experience of curriculum projecteering would suggest that objective learning theories would be treated with more circumspection, and there ought to be much more scope for heuristic teaching methods. The course would be integrated science as science; flirtations with social studies and humanities are irrelevant. The way to make science more interesting is to borrow not the content of these areas, but their more enterprising pedagogy. And this would follow from the approach I have outlined, because it would give a central place to the nature of scientific thinking and process, and so shift the emphasis away from things and towards people. It seems extraordinary that the richness, colour and humanity of the history of science, and of scientific ideas, are almost completely ignored in school science courses whether orthodox or innovatory. Science teachers are sitting on the lid of a treasure chest, which would transform their subject into one of enlivening discussion and investigation rather than of formal exposition and inert facts. And alongside this main course, the optional extra course in years 4 and 5 would perhaps be based on a project approach, bringing out both the differences and similarities between the separate subjects and covering areas of content and concept as a preparation for A-level work.

This is a far-reaching proposal, and does not overlook the inventive and thoughtful teaching which the combination of curriculum projects, staff commitment and energetic LEA science advisers has wrought in a number of schools. And the initiatives of the Association for Science Education (and its predecessors) are matched by those of the Association of Teachers of Mathematics and the enterprise and conviction of the SMP. But the reforms in both these key curriculum areas have their roots in the early 1960s. Since then we have learnt much about curriculum design and implementation, and much too about comprehensive education. Although there is now no financial flood tide for new projects to catch, as there was then, the need for an evaluation and reconstruction from first principles, so that mathematics and science can enjoy the opportunites the common culture curriculum will offer, should become an unmistakeable imperative for which funds should be found. In the meantime, I have indicated in Chapter 4 how a serviceable programme can be mounted successfully in each of these areas by using courses and materials presently available.

But such an approach places additional demands on staff, and this is true too in modern languages teaching, where professional associations have shown little curriculum vigour, and the impact of very expensive projects has, if anything, served only to tighten the grip of French as the first language, at the expense of German at first remove, but ultimately of Spanish, Russian, Chinese and Latin in the second place. The difficulties with foreign language teaching stem from three sources: conservatism and confusion among many language teachers; uncertainty regarding the aims and extent of such studies; and a failure to place language teaching and its pedagogy coherently in the context of the comprehensive school.

One would hesitate to suggest the expenditure of even more money on language curriculum studies, even though there is a case for it. But a better approach might be through school-based in-service education, providing it is conceived not just as a shot in the arm for languages teachers, but also as part of a more far-reaching study which relates languages teaching to the whole curriculum. We must also keep a sense of proportion about foreign languages. To validate the performance of a school by counting the number of pupils obtaining passes in English, mathematics, a science and a foreign language, as is sometimes advocated, is to give foreign languages an importance which is not justified either on a view of liberal education, or on available information regarding their commercial value; and more seriously, it is to ignore the overriding importance of motivation in their study at any age. Let us see more realistic demands made on schools, and an approach which puts modern languages energetically but sensitively in the context of a common curriculum.

I have looked at three important subjects which are frequently exposed both to pedantry and punditry. I should like now to consider briefly the place on the curriculum of the comprehensive school of three which tend to come in for less attention, but whose role seems to be uncertainly defined. There is first home economics, which aspires to greater curriculum significance since the old days of domestic science. To look at Schools Council Curriculum Bulletin 4 (1971), you might think that there are few areas of the curriculum which could not be dealt with in a home economics classroom. It is, in truth, an odd mixture of straight-forward cookery skills (which, in practice, predominate), along with opportunities for work in social education and even science (as food chemistry, or in product evaluation). And in its organisation and procedures, there is a useful component of personal management and discrimination which is not always evident in other areas of the curriculum. As a part of an inter-related art and craft course, it is perhaps only the latter element which is of value; otherwise its presence is a matter of administrative convenience, so that all pupils can have some experience of cooking and household management as a basic instrumental aim. For the first three years this ought to be presented as a mandatory element, and not as an optional activity. It would then be offered as an examination course in the fourth and fifth years, where in many comprehensives it seems to become a recognised way of diverting girls who have little motivation or career aim. My experience suggests that where a demanding common curriculum achieves a high engagement with all pupils, reducing the need for a plethora of options, it is a subject with a definite but limited vocational appeal. There may be some over-provisioning for it in many schools.

On the other hand, as I have suggested in Chapter 3, it might make sense to include it as part of a humanities provision, and this would bring its social education aspect into more prominence, although possibly at the expense of the cookery component. The message here is, I think, that rational curriculum planning would consider the place of the subject in the whole curriculum of the individual school, and decide exactly where it could most effectively operate, and with what kind of curriculum programme. Its role at present seems to be very variable and all too often rather unsatisfactory.

I have already emphasised the important contribution drama can make as a mandatory element of, perhaps, the expressive faculty in a common curriculum. Yet so often it is either an option in years 4 and 5, or associated with courses for children who are labelled non-academic. Or, if it is a compulsory element in the first three years, it is seen as an isolated slot, not linked in with any other area and perhaps, as a result, not particularly well done. If its potentialities for aesthetic, social and moral education were recognised, heads would get together with drama staff to take a closer look at what was happening, and see it as an essential curriculum component for pupils of all abilities. Here again, the vital move is to look at the whole curriculum and plan on the basis of an educational brief rather than individual subjects.

Finally, there is the sad story of curriculum music, which shares its unpopularity with French and religious education. I have outlined a new role for RE in some detail in Chapter 4, as part of a humanities faculty; and suggested that music benefits from interrelation with English and drama. But there has been a regrettable failure to consider the curriculum contribution of music, and this contrasts sharply with the enthusiasm shown by LEA advisers for county youth choirs and orchestras, which have no more to do with curriculum music than the international olympiad has to do with curriculum maths. But they are prestigious, and vastly more fun than improving the classroom initiation of all pupils into music as an aesthetic activity. Yet there are many philosophers of education who would see it as a vital component of aesthetic understanding, and a number of helpful suggestions for its curriculum role are made by Whitfield (1971), based on the Phenix analysis, where it is seen as a component also of symbolics, symmetrics, ethics and synoptics.

Such curriculum development as has taken place in music has, as usual, been bounded by a narrow subject-centred view, without benefit of a wider field of vision. Indeed, Schools Council Working Paper 35 narrowed its view still further, to music and the young school-leaver. Classroom initiatives seem to have been born of desperation rather than cognitive planning, with an emphasis on the creative element without an adequate sense of what it can lead to as part of a five-year course. The result can be a feeling of *déjà vu* setting in with pupils, an inadequate basis of notational skills, and a heavy bill in damaged chime bars and broken piano strings. In this area, improved pedagogy and a meaningful curriculum role will go hand-in-hand with better in-service education and thorough school-based curriculum planning.

Chapter 8

The Sixth Form

Self-generated, rather than externally imposed, change in education can take an extraordinarily long time to become institutionalised. Attempts to force the pace can easily misfire, as the Schools Council have discovered with their proposals for a common system of examination at 16-plus. Indeed, Voege (1975), from a study of the time it has taken Keynesian economics to penetrate American college and high-school textbooks, agrees with other researchers that 'schools tend to adopt ideas about twenty to twenty-five years after they first become available'. If Voege is right, the common culture comprehensive curriculum will have arrived by 2001, in time for export to any other interested planets.

The story of English sixth-form reform may yet confirm this time-scale too, for Schools Council Working Paper 5, on sixth-form curriculum and examinations (1966), opens with the news that 'At its first meeting in October 1964, the Schools Council decided that priority should be given . . . to a study of sixth form curriculum and examinations.' And as I write, it is reported that the Council is about to revive its 1971 proposals for the five-subject N and F structure, in the hope that they could be implemented by 1984. If this were to happen – and few teachers not on the Council (and there are some) would give it more than an outside chance – it would put a twenty-year price on the priority label.

But externally imposed change can be as swift as a knife in the back, to judge by the fate of so many colleges of education in the last few months. This is particularly likely if the root cause is economic rather than political, and it is widely believed that economic pressures will see off the school sixth form just as surely as they have traditional patterns of teacher education. Few comprehensive-school sixth forms get into three figures, and many languish with a lot less. Almost certainly, provision for the individual school sixth form of less than about 100 can only be adequate at the expense of provision for the first five years. At first sight, there is a reasonable case on educational grounds for at least inter-school sixth-form links, and perhaps for concentrating the provision in one school of a group. And the economic case for the sixth-form or tertiary college, which absorbs most or all of the 16–19 education in a given area, looks even more titillating to both the DES and the cost-conscious LEA.

There is a bit more, though, in both arguments, and on both sides. While the comprehensive, unlike the traditional grammar school, will not see the sixth form as the summit and flower of its achievement, I have myself seen, in watching a school grow, how benign an influence the sixth form's presence can exert for a sense of educational continuity and for civilised values. I am sure there are few 11–16 schools which would pass up the chance of their own sixth-form if it were offered. As a general principle, the notion of an educational continuum seems sensible, and seems most likely to prosper if the number of different institutions is as few as possible. But it can be argued that change offers social advantages, and it has been reported that a forthcoming NFER study will show that fears that a break at 16 will mean fewer children from working-class families staying on are not justified. The advocates of all-in tertiary colleges would claim, too, that the distinction between school-based 16–18 provision and the further education sector is undesirable, and its elimination opens up wider educational possibilities. Some schemes of reorganisation have, in fact, recognised the weight of this argument to some extent by school-college link schemes, with shared timetables allowing fluid movement between A-level, O-level and OND courses.

The economics of the sixth-form or tertiary college solution are both more tempting and yet less penetrable. It is certainly not self-evident that the establishment of a separate institution will be cheaper, in all areas of the country, than schemes based on links between schools and colleges. But it would be unwise to assume that any 11–18 school can regard its sixth form as a continuing presence for the next ten years, as for the last ten. It is therefore that much more important to consider, as I shall in this chapter, the most effective and economical ways in which it can be given adequate provision with the least disturbance to a common curriculum in the first five years. And although I shall discuss possible changes in its examination structure, it seems sensible to assume that A-level, O-level and CSE will be the basis of the programme in the foreseeable future.

The fundamental sixth-form problem is of breadth versus depth. This is conventionally seen as general studies versus examinations, but Schools Council Working Paper 45 (1972) rightly saw it in wider terms:

> Take a sixth-former with known abilities and attainments, and with . . . an immediate objective: can we devise a [curriculum] formula . . . which, while seeing that his particular talents and his particular aims are looked after, contains all the elements necessary for a balanced education? The answers may lead us to a traditional, subject-based curriculum or they may not.

We can recognise the question posed as Eisner's first dilemma of curriculum-making. Working Paper 45 goes on to propose a solution in terms of subjects, but not a traditional one. Instead of a vocational core of three A-level exam subjects, with a side-dish of mind-broadening general studies, it advocates a five-subject examination, with three at a substantially lower level, but all five presenting coverage of the elements of a balanced curriculum.

Given the present status quo, schools have no alternative but to devise ways of breathing life-enhancing balance into a curriculum composed of familiar ingredients. But it would be wrong to assume that any of the various reforms that have been proposed in the last ten years or so would necessarily make the task easier, whatever the intention. They have not been adopted, simply because the suggested cure has been generally reckoned worse than the disease. Not only has the three A-level structure support from the universities; it appears, from a study by Taylor, Reid and Holley (1974), that teachers markedly prefer the three subjects with general studies type of curriculum to any of five alternatives, for intending university students. A survey by Holley (1975) suggests that while students would like a broader education in the sixth form, they would prefer it to be done by raising the standard of general studies courses.

The present A-level, O-level, general studies mix must therefore be regarded as very durable, and schools usually claim it enables them to offer a broadly based education. But a recent extensive survey of general courses in sixth forms by the General Studies Association (1976) has revealed that the majority of sixth-forms do not offer a wide range of non-examination work. 'If PE and craft courses are removed, the only area of work most of them offer comes under the heading of arts.' Furthermore, although 60 per cent of the schools in the survey claimed to have a common core course, 'it emerged on closer inspection that most of these thought that PE, RE and "balancing subjects" (e.g. arts for scientists) together constituted a common core.' We have, however, noted earlier that many comprehensives offering the traditional multiple-option scheme in the fourth and fifth year have managed to convince themselves that theirs is a common curriculum. It is no surprise to find the same talent for self-delusion applied to the sixth.

If a school undertakes to broaden its sixth-form curriculum by making general studies a coherent common core, there are important questions to be faced, and all the staff should be invited to face them. For such a programme will impose an additional constraint on the timetable, and adapting to it may well dislocate in some way the arrangement of the examination work, and thus affect sooner or later almost all the staff. Unless a consensus can be established at the beginning the new scheme will eventually come unstuck. If there is a compulsory core, how much of it is needed? How can its content be decided? How can it be made attractive and important to pupils? These are fundamental questions which could ideally, perhaps, be answered at a staff conference.

It is interesting to note that at Sheredes School, such a conference held two years before our first pupils entered the sixth form resulted in unanimous endorsement of the principle that the sixth-form curriculum should pursue the same objective of a broad general education for all pupils that is the aim of that over the first five years. And although its implementation has involved a new view of the formal contact period, and involved staff in additional off-timetable commitments for some pupils, support for the scheme has not wavered.

Each school will make its own interpretation of a balanced curriculum for the 16–19 range. Balance for each individual student, in the sense of a personal diet that will cover distinct knowledge areas, is hardly possible in a three A-level context, and is likely to be awkward in some cases even with the five-subject scheme of Working Paper 45. And in any case, the concept will not have the same meaning from 16 to 19 as it does from 11 to 16. For those five years, education is a statutory provision, and to see it as offering all pupils access to our culture is both to discharge a duty, and to allow them to discover their own strengths. Thereafter, whether at school, at college or at work, we accept that they will more closely bring into focus those studies and activities which appeal to them. But we are anxious that the idea of continuing education should not be lost; and in the sixth form we want to prepare them for adult decisons and ensure that their understanding is not exclusively confined to too narrow a field. This seems less a case for a mandatory spread between five examination subjects, and more a case for an enrichment approach centred on a worthwhile general area of study, which can be seen as complementing the examination courses of all students.

This suggests that general studies could be thought of as a two-tier scheme, with optional elements around a common core. In a survey of general studies, Randall (1976) suggests that the time allocation to them is generally considered in schools to be right at about 20 per cent of the timetable for conventional A-level students, and about 25 per cent for those on one-year or reduced A-level courses. If, therefore, three 70-minute periods out of 20 are set aside for 'central studies' as the common core, an extra one or two choice-based periods of general studies can be added on an individual basis. Provision for these will reflect staff availability; the main task will be to plan and staff well the central studies component.

While the content of such a course is likely to be seen in terms of contributions from distinct curriculum areas, there are good practical reasons for organising it thematically using a team of staff. This, in any case, is bound to be an attractive option in a school which has successfully exploited such approaches in the first five years. Working Paper 45 grouped 8 elements under 4 headings: communication skills, cognitive, affective and expressive. This is a bizarre scheme, probably owing more to a psychological than a philosophical perspective, and likely to cause confusion in, for example, its mysterious separation of 'moral and aesthetic sensibility', as 'affective', from the 'cognitive' area of 'knowledge and understanding'. A better basis might well be derived from the faculty areas established in the first five years as an interpretation of liberal education. Four broad areas would then be: expressive arts; maths and science; design; and humanities. A topic like 'conflict' might then map onto these areas as, respectively: a study of war literature; biological warfare leading to genetics; conflicting styles in art; race relations, leading to a historical study of conflict. A fifth area might conveniently tackle sociological, philosophical and moral issues; in this case, perhaps, a sociological case study of a family, leading to work in linguistics. The detailed format can then be developed by the central studies team, with a staffing ratio of one teacher to every 10 or 12 sixth-formers. The emphasis would be on a variety of approaches, so as to give the best chance of looking at issues from a variety of aspects, and of structuring the students in a variety of ways. Films, slides, lectures by visiting speakers, outside visits, debates and discussion groups can be used, along with information and study sheets and any other published materials which can serve as a source of ideas or evidence. Some of the packs produced by the Schools Council General Studies Project can be useful here, as can a school's parents, who will represent a cross-section of society and occupations and who will be glad to help with talks and visits. Other themes for consideration might be: Aspects of a technological society; Crime; Democracy; The Shrinking Earth.

Planning such a course needs to go on well in advance, and it will need a budget allocation, some facility for software storage, and ideally a coordinator, too, who may well have to combine such a task with other academic or pastoral responsibilities. But it is by no means an immensely demanding affair to mount, and experience of such a course confirms that the coherence it brings to general studies is appreciated by students. An outline proposal for a similar scheme has been made by Gilbert and Egginton (1976), based on Phenix's realms of meaning, which are converted into five areas for a general studies core course: Communication; Our world; Man as a creator; Relationships; and Self and society.

It is convenient in practice to plan the course as a five-term continuum for all students in both lower and upper sixths. This leaves the summer term of the second year free for the upper sixth to attend to A-level examinations, and prevents repetition. But in any event, it is easy to introduce a topic for the upper or lower sixth only if circumstances favour this. Another useful device is to use a member of the standing team to release a teacher who can make a unique contribution to the work on some topic. Since the team will be drawn from representative faculties, this is possible without too much disruption providing it is prepared for in advance. Thus, if the head of languages is a member of the central studies team, he could stand in for the classicist in his department and free him to join central studies during the week when Plato's view of education is under discussion. As always, a team approach offers the most flexibility.

The general studies provision will be rounded off by other optional periods, which might include: games and recreational activities; art and craft courses; a drama option; and single periods in topics based on particular staff enthusiasms, like astronomy or war games. A period for careers topics will be compulsory during the first term each year, and will be organised by the careers education staff. Thereafter this period could continue as an option based on consumer affairs. Alternatively, topics of this kind might preferably be incorporated in the common core.

Let us see now how such a provision can run alongside that for examination courses. It has been planned as a basic core provision, which can be expanded to meet the needs of one-year sixth-formers, or those on two-year courses but taking only one or two A-levels. The same degree of adaptability is needed in planning O-level, CEE and A-level courses, but it must be achieved without excessive use of scarce resources. A-level courses can be particularly expensive to staff, especially in the early years when a sixth form is becoming established but set numbers are low. It is a fact that over 80 per cent of all entries are accounted for by these ten subjects, in descending order of popularity: English, mathematics (single subject), physics, history, geography, chemistry, economics, French, biology, art. To these many schools might like to add German, Latin, home economics, sociology, music, woodwork and metalwork; but provision in these secondary subjects might well be seen increasingly as a matter for inter-school cooperation. A second A-level mathematics subject is unlikely where SMP is adopted all through, but will be needed if traditional pure and applied mathematics are established. In short, 12 or 14 subjects will meet most needs, both of students and of staff in establishing, say, a tradition of two modern languages to university entrance level. Set size will vary from as few as 5 to as many as 20 students, and in a popular subject like English with many essays to be read, two sets may be needed as sixth-form numbers near the 80 mark.

There is a surprising variety of provision when we come to the time allocated to A-level subjects, and little available information. An intuitive judgment is that most schools see seven 35-minute periods or equivalent as the basic requirement, with an extra one or two periods to allow for practical work in science subjects. Whether this represents under- or over-teaching depends on the attitudes the students bring to their A-level work, and this in turn will depend on the approach to learning that has been fostered in the first five years. A 1970 Schools Council survey of sixth-form pupils and teachers discovered that half of Britain's sixth-formers find the transfer from the fifth form difficult. Over half admitted that they did not make the best use of their private study time. One teacher who was reported as saying 'One thing they find difficult is the change from O-level, when they have all the facts presented, to a different type of study where they are expected to ferret out facts and ideas for themselves', perhaps put his finger on the general cause. For the conventional subject-based curriculum largely derives its learning objectives from the O-level syllabuses, and there is consequently a great emphasis on rote learning and recall rather than inquiry and understanding.

The skills of inquiry will be an essential tool for the student in a common curriculum from 11 to 16, and the assessment of course work in some of the 16-plus examinations develops self-reliance and powers of organisation. Furthermore, the whole style of pupil-teacher relations is one which will foster maturity and self-knowledge. It is important, though, that the value of recalled knowledge and intellectual precision is not overlooked, for these are going to matter to all pupils, and especially those going on to A-level work. If we are optimistic about the benefits of a broad curriculum, based on a thorough rationale, in years 1 to 5, it seems reasonable to allocate three 70-minute periods to each A-level subject, with an additional fourth for each science subject. This makes good sense if Nuffield A-levels in physics, chemistry and biology are used, and these follow on remarkably well from SCISP.

We can, however, go further, and consider how these three periods will be used. Should they be seen as formal contact time, just as in the first five years? Or is it reasonable to suppose that, since A-level pupils will have higher education and the professions in mind, some move might be made in the direction of personal tuition and more informal groupings? The three periods might then be seen as two of formal timetabled lessons in the usual pattern, and one which would not be timetabled (although, of course, part of a teacher's total load) but which could be used in a variety of ways: individual supervisions; small-group discussion; or parts of the group at different times, including, if the teacher preferred, at lunch time or after period 4. Such an approach bespeaks a more mature view of proceedings, on the part of both staff and students; but it seems a not inappropriate one for the sixth form. There is the further advantage, too, that it introduces a valuable element of timetable flexibility, which greatly helps offset the extra constraint of a common core general studies component. Support for this concept of the 'tutorial period' would, of course, have to come from all the staff; but if it is seen in the context of a coherent programme, my experience is that it would be gladly given.

Thus each 2-year three A-level student will have between 9 and 12 A-level periods, including tutorials (the higher figure for all-in scientists) and about 4 general periods, including of course central studies. This leaves between 4 and 7 private study periods, some of which can, at a tutor's discretion, be diverted to O-level courses. For these a basic allocation of 2 periods each seems adequate, and they are essentially a lower sixth provision: either as re-takes or extras for A-level students, or as a study core for one-year sixth-formers. The Certificate of Extended Education (CEE) was established with the latter group in mind, and makes a useful basis for a course in some subjects, particularly in mode 3. But some of the mode 1 courses may be even more demanding than O-level, because of an excessive emphasis on content. Although its formal recognition is still delayed, and generally it is not a particularly successful new entrant in the unending examination field, it is none the less an advantage that a pass in its first two or three grades is acceptable as equivalent to an O-level pass. It remains for staff to devise mode 3 approaches which exploit the opportunities to move away from the formality of O-level. There will, though, be scope for introducing O-levels not met in the fifth year, and if there are mode 3 O-level or CSE examinations in the fifth, then new exams will be needed anyway. In practice this is not at all a disadvantage, since it rings the changes, for the student, on what would otherwise be over-familiar territory.

Altogether, about nine or ten O-level/CSE courses should be sufficient. There might be CSEs in English, based on local history; environmental studies (although the London O-level may be more adaptable); and English, where pupils taking the 2-period course can be entered, with skilful CSE mode 3 planning, either for CSE or O-level at the end of the year. Other O-level subjects could be: French, geography, geology, mathematics (with some Christmas re-takes), sociology and statistics. In most cases, the principle of one timetabled period plus one tutorial can be applied. And in particular cases, like environmental studies, the group may be large and the provision might advisably be increased to a double period (to facilitate fieldwork) with a geographer plus a third period from the chemistry department. In order to make the best use of staffing resources, the curriculum planning must reinforce the general scheme with *ad hoc* opportunism and, in the last stages of timetabling, an awareness of how to spread the jam as evenly as possible between the various interests of the sixth form.

Individual timetables can then be constructed by stipulating a minimum load of at least 6 study units as well as central studies, allowing 2 units for an A-level and 1 for an O-level or CSE. It makes sense to invite a member of staff to act as tutor for each group of 12 or 15 students, drawn from both years; along with a year tutor who will have a general pastoral role, and also, in conjunction with the careers department, have an overview of the academic programmes of the students. This is a particularly key activity during the summer term, when returning fifth years are determining their outline programmes, and close liaison with the timetabler is essential. It will be necessary too at (and before) the beginning of the autumn term, to finalise choices in the light of the 16-plus results. It helps to produce a brochure after Christmas in the fifth year, outlining the sixth-form programme and summarising the nature of the course for central studies and for each examination subject.

Students will also be encouraged to take up leadership roles in the whole school, and here the initiative and inventiveness of the sixth-form tutors will be valuable. Their own sixth-form staff/student committee will be helpful, particularly in promoting community links and aiding community projects. Some will opt for a tutorial function with lower-school forms; others help remedial pupils by hearing them read; others help with the school bookshop, summer fete, stationery shop and library. There will also be scope with clubs and societies and in organising team games.

These leadership roles must not be confused with the policing duties generally assigned to sixth-form prefects. This is an objectionable concept, for two reasons. First, once a school invents prefects, it also invents non-prefects; we are back with them and us, and it is difficult to see how the pattern of fraternal inter-dependence and responsibility discussed in Chapter 5 can be constructed if a distinction is made between pupils who are 'trusties' – whatever their age – and the others. And second, it is by no means clear that sixth-formers are competent to make disciplinary judgments and mete out punishments in the whole-school context. These are matters which call for sensitivity, experience and understanding. No doubt a few sixth-formers will have some of these qualities; they are unlikely to have them all. When we look for maturity and depth of humanity in teachers, we do so because they will underpin all the judgments teachers make. Whether one is analysing the causes of the French Revolution, or seeing that pupils use the staircases sensibly in afternoon break, these qualities are needed in schools. They may not be needed in controlling the movement of humanity in army huts or prisons, because these institutions are concerned with training, not education. The traditional prefect concept is based on a misunderstanding of the totality of school as an educational experience.

To say, however, that sixth-formers are not yet adults is but to say we must do all we can to initiate them into the maturity they will be expected to show as 18-year-old voters. There is much to be said for a separate sixth-form centre, whether purpose-built or not. Ideally it should perhaps be near enough to the school complex to be part of it, but separate enough to give it a distinct identity. There will be facilities for coffee and refreshments on a self-help basis, and the layout of the space might recognise three common modes of using free-period time: for straightforward socialising round coffee and chat; for low-key academic work, with discussion and perhaps music; and high-pressure work in complete silence. The sixth form may well have to share part of their accommodation for part of the time, perhaps with the fifth form for lunches, perhaps with the expressive arts faculty, of which their accommodation might be a separated annexe. This is perhaps a good thing, since the feeling of limited association with the whole school, of a conditional rather than a prescriptive link, is one which is likely to generate the best vibrations. Tutors and other staff will be welcome to come in for coffee after lunch, and will probably transact much of their business that way. The general style will, in fact, be much closer to the informality of the FE college than the fussy isolation of the old grammar school. And it will have a quality further education institutions seem to lack; a warmth in the relations between student and teacher, and understanding that their mutual involvement goes beyond the vocational transaction to the more personal values that lie at the heart of education.

The scheme I have outlined is based on the present state of examination play. I should like now to return briefly to the proposals for reform that have been made, and look at them in the light of the concept of balance. It will be recalled that the Schools Council's N and F plan will require a pass at 18-plus in 5 subjects: three at N-level, which requires half the study time of a normal A-level, and two at F-level, requiring three-quarters of the time. Holley (1975) has pointed out that this scheme falls into the common trap of assuming that a 'broader curriculum' means 'more subjects'. As a result, Holley argues, 'the debate has focused too narrowly on the number of subjects in the curriculum, with considerations about the range of subjects often added as an afterthought, and with little or no consideration given to developments within subjects, and the development of "new subjects".' This is an interesting line of thought which deserves further consideration. It is true that the old Higher School Certificate was not constructed on a single-subject basis, and the OND and HND are examples of course-based curricula. If the notion of the balanced curriculum were taken outside the context of separate single subjects, it would also be possible to introduce an element of unity which will be lacking in any compensatory general studies scheme, and which is difficult to perceive in the N and F proposals, although Working Paper 45 identified the need for what was termed an 'integratory' aspect to the curriculum.

There are those who would see this as supporting a move towards the International Baccalaureate, and others who would argue we should go further and consider the development of inter-disciplinary curriculum components. These matters are outside my scope here. But such components are, of course, often found in university courses, and we have found them convenient in developing a common culture curriculum in the first five years of a comprehensive school. Seen in this perspective, a preoccupation in the sixth-form curriculum with isolated subjects looks to be out of kilter. It would seem to be important, in devising new schemes, to look not just at the sixth form, but at the whole pattern of 16–19 provision and at the kind of experience of, for example, modular courses which some institutions are developing for the Diploma in Higher Education. It may well be, too, that the experience of schools in developing common culture curricula for 11–16 pupils will throw a useful light on more ingenious ways in which studies can proceed in depth while retaining the element of breadth which common sense suggests is desirable.

At the present time, though, it is as likely that the Schools Council's N and F proposals will advance further as it is unlikely that any attempt will be made to look at the sixth form and its examinations in the wider 16–19 context. It is certainly an achievement to secure any change in the present pattern; Peterson (1973) considered it the sector most resistant to change, adding 'how else can one account for the extraordinary way in which the sixth form in this country has survived in spite of all the changes around it?' But one answer is that, quite simply, schools, staff and students like the mix of Advanced Level and general subjects. It is undoubtedly true that the general education aspects are skimped all too often; but it is also true that the mix offers enough flexibility to allow a good job to be made of these aspects if a school puts its mind to it. The N and F scheme prescribes curriculum breadth by examination, which reduces flexibility and may mean that some students get less general education than under a well-run scheme of the present kind. And its emphasis on subjects is philosophically not easy to justify, as Barrow's study (1976) could be taken to suggest. But it should put a stop to the more excessive A-level cramming practices which are possible under the present arrangements, and will breathe new life into minority subjects like classics and modern languages. On balance, we must raise two cheers for it.

Chapter 9

School, Pastoral Care and Community

There are some educationists and teachers who would maintain that the relationships between the school, its community, the child, and his parents – a complex four-way interaction – are of prime importance, and should therefore be discussed in the first chapter rather than the last. Some would go so far as to say that school as an institution is almost incidental to a learning process which they would prefer to locate in the family and the community; others would, at any rate, suggest that the school is seen by the pupil first as a 'caring community', and only secondly as a place of learning, on the grounds that the second cannot occur satisfactorily without the first.

We can certainly accept that if a pupil feels insecure at school, and senses it to be a place of indifference and perhaps rejection, then he is not likely to learn very much. But he may not learn much, either, in a milieu which cocoons him in a cosy framework based on his own view of the curriculum he would like, designed to respond to his changing wants and needs rather than an intentional process of learning experiences. Discovery, as Bruner has said, favours the prepared mind. Knowledge and understanding do not just seep into our brains under the action of some irresistible osmotic pressure. Although, for example, there must be few adults who fail to see a daily newspaper or watch a television news bulletin, sampling surveys always reveal that very few politicians and public figures can be given a name by most of the population.

We can agree, too, that a school which discourages contact with parents, fails to discuss their children's progress or difficulties with them, and sees itself as an exclusive fastness remote from the cares and concerns of everyday life, will not attract their support and may even drive a wedge between them and their children. This kind of polarisation has been documented by Lacey (1970):

> The sort of friends the boy makes and the attitude he develops to his work are radically affected by polarisation, and are matters that concern his parents far more directly than the technical pedagogical arguments. Parents' ability to interfere with this process on their children's behalf is related to their ability to present the problem in terms of the school's ideology, and is linked to social class.

But again, if our proper revulsion at such wrongheadedness leads us to argue that the school must construct its educational programme out of the values and aspirations of its parents and their community, we will deny their children access to the full richness of our culture. In a working-class area, there will be little incentive to look beyond immediate necessities and satisfactions at the world of ideas and abstractions; and in many middle-class areas the life of the mind will be just as remote, driven out by a preoccupation with O-level passes in French and mathematics at the expense of an understanding of aesthetics and the social sciences, and indeed anything which cannot be equated with a high-income career.

It is therefore essential to avoid the glib over-simplification, the challenging extreme of argument, and recognise that the absolute educational good is very hard to discover. However tempting the rhetoric may be, there is no royal road. As Ben Morris wrote, in Schools Council Working Paper 12:

> Education is an enterprise with values built into it by its very nature. More and more these values have to be the results of conscious choices rather than of tradition . . . As educators we have to try to take rational decisions in terms of what we value most.

But the process of choice and decision depends on our own judgment, and perhaps serves to remind us, looking back at our own education, of the need to have that broad background of general education which can lead us to autonomous action. Writing in *The Times* (18 October 1975) of his memories of Oxford in 1912 as an undergraduate, Harold Macmillan recalled the opening lecture of a course by a celebrated professor of moral philosophy:

> Gentlemen – you are now about to embark upon a course of studies which will occupy you for two years. But . . . nothing that you will learn in the course of your studies will be of the slightest possible use to you in after life, save only this: that if you work hard and intelligently you should be able to detect when a man is talking rot, and that in my view, is the main, if not the sole, purpose of education.

As Macmillan remarks, there have been worse definitions.

Let us look at the relations between the pupil and the school, bearing in mind that an over-readiness to take up positions of conventional piety at one extreme or the other has led to much rot being talked on the subject. The first thing to say is that the pupil's feelings of social self-respect and security will stem from the way the school brings him into that process for which it exclusively exists – the process of teaching and learning. And this is why I make no apology for giving absolute priority to questions of education, curriculum and culture. In doing so, we must always have in our minds a picture of children in schools, and the ways in which they can be led to ask the right questions about the various elements of our culture; but we must not allow our judgments of the meaning of education, and of the selection from our culture, to be clouded by questions which are at root social or psychological rather than philosophical. If our techniques and strategies are unequal to some of the resulting tasks, we must modify or adapt, while we learn to get better at these tasks. And we must recognise that our view of culture is not absolutely determined, and is bound to reflect new knowledge and new societies. But the main concern of school is with cognitive and not social processes, although to recognise their close interdependence is of the first importance.

This is why non-streaming is sometimes seen as an end rather than a means. It is an understandable view, and it is difficult to think of the streamed or banded comprehensive school as any less incongruous than a Nash terrace with a thatched roof. The man on the Clapham omnibus knows that comprehensive education is to do with social justice, and sorting pupils out on the basis of dubious judgments about their abilities is fundamentally unjust. But in education it is easy to do the right thing for the wrong reason, and end up in a confused state. So it is with the decision to unstream. As I have argued in Chapter 4, if the curriculum thinking is right, it will be an ineluctable step in a rational process of development; but if it is undertaken for social reasons, a school may find it has a tiger by the tail.

This is a convenient moment to take a wider look at the matter of pupil grouping. It is often forgotten that all groups – even the most rigidly streamed – are mixed-ability groups; the argument is about the width of the ability range in the group. It is also forgotten that streaming was an innovation when it was proposed by the Board of Education half-a-century ago. It is unhelpful to assume that either streaming or non-streaming is the natural way in which pupils should be grouped. But it is true that most teachers have been trained, and are still being trained, to use teaching styles which work best with streamed groups; and it is also true that to many educationists the streamed comprehensive school is a contradiction in terms.

The result is the confused state of practice outlined in Chapter 2. A recent article by Reid (*Times Educational Supplement* of 10.6.77), Principal Research Officer of the NFER Mixed Ability Teaching Project, quotes an NFER survey in 1974–5 of over 1,000 comprehensive schools which bears this out:

> just over half employed mixed ability groups as the mode of organization for most of the curriculum in the first year, 37% continued into the second year and 24% in the third. Throughout, however, fairly extensive use was made of setting for such subjects as mathematics and foreign languages. Hence, of those schools with a predominantly mixed ability organisation in the first year, 46% employed setting for some subjects; in the second year this rose to 77%; and in the third year . . . 91% used setting for some subjects.

It is clear from this very large sample that the chance that a first-year pupil in a comprehensive will have mixed ability teaching in foreign languages can only be half of 54 per cent, or slightly more than 1 in 4. It is, therefore, surprising that the HMI report on Mathematics, Science and Modern Languages (1977) can so readily assert that mixed-ability teaching is a major cause for concern in these subjects, and disturbing to find sweeping generalisations made with no attempt to substantiate them.

As Reid points out, the technical difficulties in comparing pupil performance in groups with different ability ranges are severe: 'The problem is to disentangle from an almost endless list of variables – home, school, teacher and classroom – what is relevant to a child's learning . . . Studies have frequently failed to take account of teaching content and method; the measurement of product has not been accompanied by the study of process.' Little purpose is served in making observations which are either misleading, or tell us what is surely now self-evident: that unless mixed-ability teaching is seen as part of a process of curriculum preparation and planning, it has so much stacked against it – lukewarm and untrained staff, no clear statement of objectives and procedures, inadequate resources – that only a miracle could make it succeed.

Yet the disadvantages of streaming, banding and early setting must increasingly push schools towards mixed-ability organisation. The well-known research of Rosenthal and Jacobsen (1968) shows how much performance depends upon environment. Teachers were told that one group had scored high on IQ tests, and another low, when in fact both groups were randomly assigned. But the bright group got brighter, and the slow group slower. Other evidence shows how difficult it is for pupils to move between streams, bands or sets; the disturbance it generates for the child; and the way in which assessment labels stick from primary through to the secondary school in streamed systems. And if the pupils are streamed, so often are the teachers. Further objections centre on the social and moral disadvantages of separating children into different learning milieux on the grounds of alleged differences in ability.

So it is not surprising to find so many comprehensives travelling earnestly on the road to non-streaming. But how confusing it must be for pupils to live in a school where they are non-streamed for humanities, banded for science, and setted for maths! There is no curriculum unity; there is no stability to the learning group; and there is no way in which the school can become a total influence system. And when this confusion is worse confounded by wholesale options in the later years, it is not surprising that pupil engagement is poor, and resources must be diverted from curriculum to pastoral care so as to help pupils find a sense of identity. A pupil in a rigidly streamed formal grammar school can at least get his bearings.

But the way ahead is clear. The practicality of effective non-streaming cannot be in doubt if it derives from curriculum planning (backed up by an adequate programme of in-service education) rather than blind faith and egalitarian hopes. And if it is seen as a non-streamed format, as I have suggested, with all its implied flexibility of resource and strategy, then the benefits of non-streaming are coupled with high pupil engagement and teaching effectiveness.

By the same token, it will be evident that instead of viewing knowledge as the raw material of a process of instruction external to the child, it must be seen as the basis of a subtle exchange between teacher and pupil, dependent upon honesty and respect, and responding to the teacher's rational and intuitive perceptions of the pupil's understanding and ways of learning. Here again, those who are hot for certainties, and ready to turn a phrase into a new doctrine, will talk unwisely of 'the reconstruction of knowledge at the pupil/teacher interface'. It is foolish to deny that the skilful teacher is in some ways as much a Dionysiac as an Apollonian, and is ever aware of how he must modify and bend, twist and turn so as to strike a secure lodgement in the pupil's mind for the knowledge, attitude or skill he seeks to impart. But it is just as foolish to see this process as an end in itself, and thus introduce the kind of distortion which makes a convenient peg on which to hang another exercise in pseudo-theory, but does much disservice to those who are fumbling, as we all are, to find our own glimpse of the truth about a complex process.

I have discussed the pupil-teacher relation in this context in Chapter 5, and stressed its bearing on the 'hidden curriculum'; all those events and exchanges that the pupil encounters in the school, but which are not directly connected with the curriculum as a list of approved content and prescribed method. But the connexion must be made; partly by viewing the learning process in the way I have described, which will follow from the changed role of the teacher in the innovating school; partly by establishing a system of consistent values; and partly by conscious decisions to involve the pupil in the life of the school, such as by the forum mechanism described earlier. Such decisions will involve a close look at how every element in the school day impinges on the pupil. The hypocrisy, for example, of school assemblies which use an act of worship as an opportunity to pillory those who are late or wearing the wrong uniform; a surfeit of bells, which are necessary but call for moderation; the impersonality of loudspeaker announcements; and the bestiality of pushing pupils out of the building during breaks. I have yet to hear a good reason for this abominable practice; I think it has something to do with a mistaken view of teachers' responsibilities in regard to duties. For my part, I have yet to meet a teacher who is reluctant to see his role, both in the morning and at lunch time, as extending to a reasonable surveillance of the building and its environs; providing these matters are discussed in a sensible way, as part of the school's whole process of decision-making and its whole view of education.

In many schools great importance is attached to after-school activities, and parents seem to regard them as a major test of a school's educational worth. A moment's thought is enough, though, to see that while they are desirable and necessary in some ways, they are only an adjunct to the school's real business. There may be after-school teams in every sport from rugby to rowing, and societies from mathematics to matchbox-labels; but what matters is the 300-odd minutes daily of compulsory curriculum. The sixth-form literary society looks good in the prospectus, but why are some pupils unable to start French in the first year? Last term's Shakespeare play drew packed houses, but why is drama not even an available option for clever fourth-year pupils? The truth is that if the curriculum values are right, there will be a natural efflorescence of after-school activities. But they will have little impact on many pupils, and schools exist to provide good things for all pupils. This is why the voluntary principle, whether in after-school games or in-school hobbies periods, must always be applied with circumspection.

It may operate to the disadvantage of some, and divert resources from others.

These effects will be the consequence of any undue emphasis, however well-intentioned, when viewed in isolation. Because educational decisions interact so much in a school, it is vital to see the disadvantages as well as the desirable consequences of any change, however small. And where substantial resources are involved, getting the right order of priorities needs clear thinking. There is no doubt that in many comprehensive schools, pastoral care has been seen out of perspective, and diverted teaching time and money from curriculum activities. The NFER research already mentioned shows how deficiencies in curriculum planning, leading to multiple-option schemes in the fourth and fifth year, give rise to pupil disaffection, particularly in the less able. It is then necessary to give year tutors or housemasters more time in which to deal with misdemeanours, and perhaps assistant staff to help them; while the school counsellor will need more time too, and the deputy heads and head will live from one contingency to the next. All these come expensive, and their time would be better spent on teaching, or curriculum planning, or talking to pupils rather than hunting them and punishing them. But once a pattern is established, it may need vision to track it back to its true cause, and see how curriculum malfunctioning has spread like a virus through the system, altering perceptions and responses and twisting values out of shape. And it may need decisive change, rather than gradual evolution, to get the design straight.

If teaching is going to be effective, every teacher must be in the pastoral care business, in the sense of getting to know the child and using that knowledge to initiate him into those learnings which reflect curriculum strategies. And this will be the mainspring of the child's feeling of security, of his confidence that he is valued for his own sake and respected as an individual. The teacher will in turn reflect the same values running through his dealings with other staff, and if there is a common curriculum operating through a non-streamed format, he will see how his own gifts and specialisms contribute to a self-reinforcing matrix of designed experiences. Through the assessment system, he will be formally involved, too, with each child's academic development. But there is a side to the pupil's school life to do with his use of the place as an institutional home from home, and from this spring those formal tasks of the form tutor which focus more directly – although not exclusively – on his social and personal development. Historically this is a well-established role, and one which offers the teacher the chance to look at the pupil in the school as a whole, rather than in a subject lesson. As well as helping the pupil to get himself organised, helping him make friends and dealing with the unexpected mishap, the good form-teacher will talk to his form as individuals, know who is in which school team, who has passed piano grade 4 or won a prize in the town carnival. But this is an extension, not a transformation of his role as a curriculum teacher in the innovating school. And by the same token, in a rigid, static school it may either throw the teacher into conflict with establishment values, or leave him just as aloof, unknowing and ineffectual in the formroom as in the classroom.

There will be some aspects of this role which will require the teacher to have more scope and a wider influence in the school, and it is convenient to associate these aspects with a year tutor in a system of horizontal organisation, or a housemaster in a vertical system. There will be administrative questions, to do with the arrangements for assessments, for example, or reports. Personal matters will arise, when the child will be seen in a wider context than the form, and parents will be brought into the discussion; and there will be matters of school rather than form discipline, where there is advantage in using the close link teachers with these responsibiiities will have with the pupil. In the independent boarding school, such links arise naturally with the master in whose house the boy is lodged, and so the vertical grouping of pupils into houses is both logical and powerful; indeed, the power of the housemasters, in concert, directly threatens that of the head in some public schools. But in the maintained day school the vertical link is tenuous because it is artificial; the enforced grouping of pupils across the years is a contrivance, justifiable only in the interests of competitive games. And since the spirit of competition is much the most powerful motive for playing games, then it makes sense to establish vertical 'sports groups', perhaps named after athletes or sportsmen (the choice could be made by the school forum), who will play matches against each other and figure prominently on sports day. And inasmuch as it leads to pupils of different ages getting to know each other, it brings an additional benefit.

But there is every advantage in making the pastoral link horizontally through the year group with a year tutor. For then the year tutor can get to know all his pupils by teaching them – and there is really no better way, apart from living with them in a boarding house. Furthermore, the team-taught common curriculum reinforces the pastoral identity of the year, because it will be taught academically by the year or the half-year. It is an obvious next step to give the year tutor enough autonomy to exploit this bond, and I have found that the relative inexperience of talented young staff does not prevent their making a tremendous success of this role. They will take their cues, as the pupils do, from the style and structure of the curriculum as it is reflected in the school, and for the head to find a miscreant parked at his doorstep will then be a rare event. It seems odd, and faintly old-fashioned, to make a distinction between disciplinary and pastoral matters for girls, as opposed to boys. Providing the balance of the sexes is sufficiently reflected in the total staffing of a mixed school, there seems no basis for differentiating senior appointments other than that of merit. The senior mistress looking after girls' welfare is out of time and place, although a head may find that Nurse Dugdale is at large on his governing body, and equally anxious to see him divert ancillary staff from vital curriculum support tasks into the appointment of a school matron. Unless a school is unusually remote from doctor or casualty department, there seems very little purpose in acquiring such a costly luxury. The school's own teaching and non-teaching staff are an adequate resource. The administration of aspirins should take second place to the school's educational programme; and if the teaching is interesting and effective, headaches are surprisingly less frequent.

An exception, though, will arise in the case of the small proportion of schools whose pupils are drawn from areas with particularly difficult social problems. It is usual for this to be reflected in the allocation of extra resources, and in return the school's educational concerns will extend to a substantial involvement in pastoral welfare. Year tutors or housemasters will need deputies and lighter timetables to permit a continuing programme of counselling and home visiting, and the ancillary resource will need a corresponding increase. The priorities of the area will be reflected in the curriculum planning, with a greater proportion of staff diverted to remedial problems, and a different order of priorities in devising the faculty structure. There may be a greater emphasis on English-language skills, or on humanities or social studies; and the resources for learning may need to place a greater emphasis on individualised learning techniques, or on recorded tape and visual materials rather than the written word. But the principles of the curriculum structure need not change. If it is devised in the way I have suggested, it will always respond to the school's own milieu, and if this presents exceptional difficulties, then the plan for the common curriculum must deal with them. But it will just as firmly aim to initiate pupils into key aspects of the culture that is our common heritage; the staff will devise, as the staff of any school must devise, its own set of objectives and learning strategies so as to reduce the effect of their constraints and increase the impact of their teaching.

Let us now extend our general consideration of school-pupil links to that of parental involvement. Here, the substance is more important than the shadow; I remember an article in which a head attached great significance to addressing and signing personally each letter inviting new parents to the school introductory social. This sort of thing helps to sell mail-order encyclopedias, and does no harm; but in general, time spent on pieces of paper is time not spent talking to people, and it matters far more that a head is able to drop everything to talk to a child's parents, and sees this as a higher priority than window-dressing gimmicks. A school parent-teacher association can bring nothing but good, providing the head has the modicum of political sense necessary to prevent its being associated with a caucus of parents, rather than a representative committee. A newsletter once or twice a term will tell all parents what is going on, and a programme of social and educational school and PTA functions will give them the chance to learn more about the school and meet its staff. All staff should be made aware that these events can be as valuable as formal parents' evenings. It is unusual for parents to want to talk shop; rather do they like the opportunity to meet staff as people and get an extra dimension to their knowledge of the school.

The basis for the school's formal report to parents will be the pupil assessment cards in each faculty. It is better to have one sustained, deeply informative report each year than two or three insubstantial reports, often only a list of subjects with scrawled marks or grades and a superficial comment. Little wonder that this unsatisfactory practice has given rise to the suggestion that each report should have a space for the parents' comments; for such reports are usually followed by free-for-all parents' evenings, where teachers sit like prize cattle in a market and parents circle round hoping to snatch a word and moving from queue to queue. Written communication is at times a formal necessity, and the school must make a written report. But what parents want is not a space for a line of comment; they want the opportunity to talk about their child to someone who knows him well. It is far better to see parents' evenings as an appointment with the form tutor, who should have the chance to write a substantial report on each child, and which would be sent, along with the faculty reports, to make up a folder of eight half-A4 sheets, a few weeks before the appointment. The head might well make a point of reading each report, and writing a comment on each. This will be appreciated by both parents and staff.

Each sheet in the folder will tell of a child's progress in words rather than grades and percentages, and it will answer two questions in relation to the particular faculty: To what extent has the pupil's work reached the standard he should set himself? And how does it compare with that of the whole year-group? The answers to these will be woven into the report, referring as appropriate to any available test results and any variation between subject assessments in the faculty. The form tutor will see the faculty reports (along with those for option subjects, or remedial reading) when they have been collected together by ancillary staff, and will then write an overview which takes into account his knowledge of the pupil in the context of the whole school. The year tutor will then read through each booklet before passing them to the head. Each sheet can be written cheaply in duplicate using carbon paper, and thus the school can retain a file copy, and the parents retain theirs throughout the pupil's school career.

The year tutor will also be present at the parents' evening, along with the head or deputy, so that any matters arising out of the discussion with the form tutor can be taken further. And if parents wish to discuss their child's work in some subjects additionally with the specialist staff concerned, then it is a simple matter to arrange further appointments, and indeed such a facility can be incorporated if necessary on the reply slip from the parents accepting the parents' evening appointment. This function can then become an agreeable social occasion.

This open and informative style of reporting, coupled with a friendliness in the school's relations with parents and a readiness to invite them to discuss any difficulties, will allay any fears parents might have that the school's internal records contain objectionable confidential material. This is an understandable fear, and will feed on the feeling that the school is remote and inaccessible and likely to accept second-hand judgments. But parents do not expect the school to live in their pockets, and it is a great error for schools to bite off more than they can chew. Arduous programmes of home visiting, and over-frequent parents' evenings, have a debilitating effect on all staff and simply make the school a less efficient place of education. It is, of course, true that schools serving overspill housing estates with many one-parent families and similar difficulties must divert more resources towards social involvement; but the school's staffing will take this into account. Schools are not particularly potent institutions, and must decide on the things they are qualified to do, and concentrate on doing those things well.

Our focus of attention is now taking us from parents to the wider community, and a pivot point here is the system of careers education adopted by the school. It would be a pity if the current concern with unemployment were to lead to a limited view of careers education; it should be seen not just as finding a job but in the wider context of determining a life-style. And because the careers staff will aim to foster self-knowledge and develop decision-making, it is evident that the common curriculum, with its emphasis on personal autonomy through a liberal education, will strongly reinforce careers education. These are qualities, after all, which cannot be engendered to order on the strength of a 35-minute careers period weekly; they must be seen in the context of the whole curriculum. But they can be encouraged in a careers context during the course of the third year, and it is particularly convenient if the third-year tutor has a careers responsibility. Then discussions about option choice can be based on personal knowledge, and it is a good idea to provide a display of careers literature in the third-year centre. With a common curriculum, no crucial career choice is needed at this stage: all paths can be kept open. This is a great boon which is unfortunately far from the case in most comprehensives with intrusive multiple-option schemes. But even a limited option choice will be for many pupils their first major decision. During the autumn term of the third year each pupil will be interviewed individually, and there will be frequent discussions with form tutors and year tutor. Parents can raise points in the light of the report at the parents' evening, and thus the final option decision can be the child's after consultation with staff and parents. Because only two options place little constraint on timetabling and resources, it is almost always possible to give each child both first-choice options.

During the fourth year each pupil is again interviewed by the careers staff and a careers record is begun, showing interest and ability in each school subject, health, activities in and out of school, disposition and so on. Pupils are at ease in this school-based 'conversation with a purpose' and this is a helpful preparation for later employment interviews. In the English department care is taken to introduce work on letters of application at this stage. In the fifth year there is a sharpening of focus, and curriculum time is used during the first and second terms for careers guidance in the implications of choosing the sixth form, colleges of further education or employment. Usually only one period a week will be needed, and can be taken in turn from each faculty. In addition there will be visits and discussions during lunch time and perhaps after school, and work experience courses are run during the Easter holiday.

A careers department working on these lines is a guidance unit rather than an information centre. Work is done on analysing occupations and opportunities so as to help the pupil to discriminate between the requirements of different firms. Aspects of qualifications and working conditions are examined, along with Income Tax, National Insurance, pension schemes and similar topics. In the sixth form, alternative routes to higher education will be discussed, with outside speakers and visits backed up by an extensive reference service. In both fifth and sixth years, the careers department will exploit links with local firms, and make use of the list of parents' interests compiled from their volunteered information at the time of secondary transfer. It amounts to an extensive provision, but it makes minimal demands on curriculum time, because the common curriculum both prepares the ground and eliminates pre-emptive decisions. In the conventional comprehensive, so much that passes for pastoral care in the middle school is little more than horse-trading over options, but with serious implications for the child when key subjects are dropped.

A further advantage of the common curriculum is that the first five years are seen as a continuum. In some schools a split site means an unavoidable break, but often there is a 'head of lower school' appointment for no very good reason. It may be necessary to compensate for discontinuities of this kind by additional pastoral commitment, possibly by the provision of a form period as well as the usual registration time at the beginning or end of each half-day session. But if the year-tutor system is meshed in with form tutoring and the academic programme, so that staff get to know pupils in the classroom, and form tutors perhaps move up with their charges while year tutors are anchored in that year and learn its context, then the registration provision is perfectly adequate. It is important, though, to look carefully at the role of assemblies and forums, as discussed in Chapter 5.

It is a recurring fashion to point to the evident discontinuity between primary and secondary school, and to suggest that the onus lies exclusively on the secondary school to ease this transition. I have been surprised every year, though, to learn from first-year pupils how much they enjoy the variety of teachers they meet compared with the solitary class teacher in the junior school. It is by no means self-evident that the one class–one teacher system is the ultimate refinement in primary education. It is certainly very convenient, and offers security to the young child. But in the upper years of the junior school, it places a great responsibility on the teacher to stretch the ablest and help the slowest, and to do so in a wide range of subjects. It would be helpful if the development of middle schools in some areas leads to the wider adoption in junior schools of patterns of team-teaching.

The secondary school will, of course, take steps to make the change from a small to a large school as smooth as it can. I have mentioned in Chapter 4 the ways in which faculties might adjust their internal arrangements so as to give a secure first-year link between pupil and teacher. But the first-year tutor will try to be a regular visitor to the contributory junior schools, and the head will be keen to extend liaison with them to his faculty heads and to first-year staff. It is a good idea for the head and tutor to visit the schools during the preceding summer term to meet the new pupils, and an introductory tour of the school for them and their parents, with last year's first-year volunteers acting as guides, is an excellent event on the evening before the autumn term begins.

On the whole, this seems a better scheme than inviting new pupils to see the secondary school in the summer term. It is more reassuring for them to be met on their home ground, which they have identified with for four years; and in many ways the dog days of June or July do not present the secondary school in a characteristic light. And many schools will probably have invited present and prospective parents to see the school during an ordinary working day during the autumn term, along with an evening event for prospective parents to meet staff and learn about the curriculum and organisation. Much stress is sometimes laid on the transmission of minutely detailed records about pupils between schools, and it is quite essential that the profile of a pupil's interests and achievements, along with a report from teacher and head, passes to the first-year tutor on transfer. The tutor will also gain much from talking to primary school staff, and it is always a good idea to ask parents to mention in writing any matters of note, and to follow these up at the preliminary parents' evening.

But too much emphasis can be laid on the bureaucratic transfer of information. To judge by the zeal with which this is sometimes urged upon us, one would imagine that the records are being transferred, rather than the child. There is, first, the danger that records really will be seen as more important, with their compilation taking up time, as will the testing on which they will be based; no one grows taller by being measured. Second, the sheer mass of information might obscure really important information, for instance about learning difficulties. And finally, records may lead teachers to make judgments on children as they were, rather than as they are. There is evidence that in streamed comprehensive schools, pupil attainment closely correlates with primary school assessment compared with a more divergent pattern in the non-streamed school. The reason is obvious: initial allocation to streams is made on the basis of these assessments, and the fact that there is little subsequent movement between them has been demonstrated by research here and abroad – most recently in a study of the intricately streamed comprehensives of Hessen in West Germany. We need to distinguish between information with either a positive or negative effect. Thus, we need to know that a pupil has a low reading age, since the new school must make provision from the start; but a pupil's difficulties with some mathematical concepts may be due to a poor primary school teacher rather than an inherent weakness, and labelling him as backward on transfer may be absolutely counter-productive. Changing schools means a fresh start, and too much stress on records can destroy the chance to take full educational advantage of it.

I should like finally to look at three explicit ways in which the school and the community may interact: through parental choice of secondary school, representation on governing bodies and by specific curriculum links. We must recognise first that the notion of the 'community school' is so elusive as to be almost without meaning: not even social scientists can agree on what we might take the community to be. If it means a recognition by the school that it is not an island, and must secure a broad base for its curriculum policies, then we can give it our support, as I have suggested in Chapter 3. It also makes good sense to utilise school buildings as fully as possible, and most schools will welcome the use of their facilities by adult evening classes. The school should be the organising body, and the school funds should benefit by worthwhile *pro rata* payments. In some areas, where the school can be sited, for example, in the centre of a small town, this concept can be taken further, giving the school extra buildings and the town a new heart, after the ideal of Henry Morris. But to work successfully this needs plenty of goodwill, the school in the right spot, and a distinct community with a diversity of opinions and social backgrounds.

It is, however, difficult to see how curriculum links with the community can be forged in any wholesale fashion unless, as I have discussed earlier, the school abdicates its responsibility to initiate pupils into the culture. But in many faculties there will be opportunities to make use of local resources: in science, humanities, mathematics, creative activities and in careers. Recently it has been argued that 'civics' should be a compulsory curriculum subject. This was a notable failure in the secondary modern school, and it is not surprising to learn that the massive survey of 21 countries published in 1976 by the International Association for the Evaluation of Educational Achievement has shown that the widely shared aim of producing aware, informed, critical and actively participating democratic citizens cannot be fully achieved by classes in civics. The reason is clear; these matters must be seen partly in terms of a social studies curriculum component, partly by reflecting them in the style of the school's organisation and the shared attitudes it represents. Only a common curriculum, underpinned by careful and rational planning, will give pupils access to these experiences as their maturity grows over the five years of compulsory schooling. Again, consistent values matter: games teachers sometimes, for example, bring pressure to bear on pupils to give up after-school or Saturday-morning jobs. But these are valuable ways in which the adolescent can get inside the adult world, and see the community from another angle; it is nice if a school can attract good support for Saturday games, but applying moral pressure is really miseducational in its broad sense.

The wide support that the school will seek for its curriculum policies will virtually begin with that of the governing body, whose articles of government at present, in most cases, give it substantial curriculum control. A detailed discussion of the likely outcome of the Taylor Committee is outside my scope, but it must be recognised that to provide subtle yet effective power sharing in education is not easy. As Kogan (1976) has written:

> The governance of education is peculiarly difficult to get right for it has to meet conflicting criteria. Efficiently run schools need competent management and professional support and control. They have to encourage teacher professionalism and participation and they have to be democratically accountable.

Although the present arrangements can lead to the appointment of good party members rather than people with a genuine educational interest, any other scheme will be open to manipulation of some sort, and enlightened authorities have taken steps to widen governor representation. It would be a sad day for curriculum innovation if we exchanged elected councillors for hidebound trade unionists, middle-class do-gooders or myopic shopkeepers, ending up with an unwieldy body which took two hours to agree on whether the school tuckshop should sell cheese biscuits. The innovating comprehensive needs a strong and coherent governing body, responsible to the elected education committee and reflecting, as Kogan puts it, democratic control rather than an atomistic form of government.

The governing body is directly concerned with the school's accountability, but parental choice is a form of accountability by stealth. In its pure form, where the measure of its success is the proportion of parents getting their first choice of school, it implies that parents are reckoned not only to know which school is best for their child, but also in effect to determine which educational programme is best, since a vote for one school is a vote against others. Some parents will make their decisions on a rational basis, touring the schools, comparing prospectuses, asking sharp questions about curriculum and examinations; their approach will usually reflect a professional experience in making value judgments. But most seem to find it an uncomfortable task, and sense it is one for which they are ill-fitted by temperament, and ill-served by school and local authority, since little useful information about the schools is usually available, and never on a comparative basis. They will rely on the judgments of their friends, or on overheard gossip, or on the choice of their child or even their child's playmates. But chiefly they will fall back on their own experience of school, and seek security by looking for what is familiar.

It follows that exclusive parental choice is a force for inertia rather than innovation. Unless the school with new ideas has assiduously tailored them and skilfully marketed them, it will end up with pupils rejected from more popular schools, which are usually reorganised former grammar schools, or conventionally streamed former secondary moderns. It may be short of numbers, and it will certainly lack abler pupils. For these are the children in general of parents who know how to work the system, and whose reasons for the first-choice school will be unbreakable. And there is a catch 22 at work too. The obvious strategy for the innovating school will be to spread the good word, and forge close links with primary schools; but this is to invite the charge of poaching, and in any case parental choice means not five contributory primary schools, but perhaps twenty-five. This of course, is a serious educational drawback in any terms; every secondary school needs to feel that it can establish curricular continuity with its own contributory schools.

The answer is not, though, to abolish parental choice, but to contain it; to let it serve educational ends rather than master them. It is, for most parents, perfectly satisfactory that their children should pass from the primary school to the comprehensive with which it is educationally linked. But some would like the option of a different school, and they should be free to make a case for it in terms which make educational sense. The officers of the authority can then adjudicate claims in the usual way, in the light of the prevailing conditions. The onus is then on the secondary school to justify its policies in the ways I have outlined, and it is regrettable that schools with secure catchment areas often do not keep this part of the bargain. Schools Council Working Paper 53 has introduced the term 'covenant' to describe this responsibility on the school's part to seek a broad basis for its policies, but it seems unnecessarily legalistic, and we may yet see the school's covenant taking its place in the head's study alongside the punishment book and governors' minutes. The spirit of a wider understanding is what matters, and it is high time pre-service and in-service education courses for heads were established on a more extensive basis so as to give incumbents a broader perspective of their role. The Inspectorate, in a recent report on ten good schools, has declared: 'Without exception the most important single factor in the success of these schools is the quality of leadership of the head.' Yet the head is almost entirely without systematised help or counsel from officers, advisers, inspectors or consultants, apart from the odd course or conference. This lamentable gap should be filled with a staff college facility, better courses and, in particular, school-based provision using a newly created team of coordinators and consultants with experience of curriculum design and implementation.

But a provision of this sort will be just as essential for all the staff of the second-generation comprehensive school. The modern industrial society changes the cultural system which forms the environment of the school, and the school's curriculum must respond to these changes. Hitherto, advisory services seem to be based on a more static view of curriculum, looking at the content rather than the context, looking at subjects rather than curriculum planning, and rarely penetrating below the protective carapace of accepted method and instant tradition. I have argued that the natural form of the comprehensive school is to operate a common culture curriculum in a non-streamed format, and that the logic of this pattern is buttressed by a view of education which is based not on historicism, and a futile search for a new, ultimate truth; but rather on the established principles of symmetry and autonomy which underpin a liberal education for our own age. I have shown how such a curriculum structure can make good use of existing subject specialisms, facilitate timetabling and promote pupil engagement. And it is capable of attracting a wide measure of support.

It also puts the teacher in a new framework. He loses old problems, but acquires new ones. But his job is more satisfying and more fulfilling, because the new problems are essentially more tractable and more congenial. The old assumption is that pupils will be bored unless something unusual happens; the new assumption is that pupils have expectations of interest, are not alienated from the school, but will demand a lively and inventive pedagogy. If the common curriculum means that the professional development of teachers will take them from a preoccupation with sticks and carrots, and a sinking feeling at the thought of the bottom third-year stream, to a process of creative curriculum action, reading, planning, working in teams and devising a set of enjoyable learning experiences; then it is surely a development only the self-satisfied time-server will fear. But talk of professional development follows, rather than precedes, curriculum planing: hence the importance of the change-agent, and the futility of the school establishing elaborate schemes of discussion and simulation when the curriculum context is left unchanged.

The overarching implication, then, is for school-focused development; and this means a focus on the individuality of both school and teacher, and a quite new approach to the nature of the support services both need. With a declining school population, it is an approach centred on in-service education, extending the skills of existing teachers rather than reducing classes, which the previously mentioned IEA survey shows does not correlate with improved quality of education. Teachers will need to look beyond their specialisms to a wider culture; beyond their own life-styles to those of other backgrounds, other interests, other professions. But as a result, the comprehensive school will come into its own, and be respected as the common school which provides an education second to none.

Appendix

Sheredes School:

Curriculum and Timetable Structure

1 Curriculum Structure: Sheredes School

		Year 1	Year 2	Year 3	Year 4	Year 5	*Subjects*	*Max.No.GCE/CSE passes*
Core	Hu	*5	5	5	5	5 →	Eng.Hist.Geog.[1]	3 (mode 3)
	EA	3	3	3	2	2 →	Eng. Music, Drama	1 (music[2])
	M	3	3	2	3	2 →	Maths	1
	CA	3	3	2	2	2 →	Design[3]	1 (mode 3)
	PA	2	2	2	2	2 →	PE. Games	
	S	2	2	3	2	2 →	Science[4]	1
	L	2	2	2 →			French	
Options	A			1				
	B				2	2	(Options subjects	1
	C				2	2	are listed below)	1

Faculties: M Mathematics; S Science; CA Creative Activities; Hu Humanities; EA Expressive Arts; PA Physical Activities; L Languages

Notes

1 Hu course also includes moral and religious education.
2 Music O-level only an adjunct and involves some after-school time.
3 An interrelated course linking art and handicraft and including housecraft.
4 One pass in Integrated Science (Mode 3 CSE). If extra science is chosen from either Option B or C (see over), then total is two passes at O-level (SCISP) or two at CSE (Human Biology, and Physics with Chemistry).

*Number of 70-min. periods, weekly. There are 4 periods daily.

OPTION A (third year)

Latin German	Introductory courses, open to all
Science Woodwork Metalwork Housecraft Art/English (linked course)	Alternative interest-based courses, peripheral to main curriculum

OPTIONS B & C (fourth and fifth year)

Option B	*Option C*
French	Extra Science
Extra Science	German(5)
Office Practice(2,4)	Latin(1)
Woodwork	Home Economics
Typing(3,4)	Metalwork
Art	Electronics(2,4)
Technical Drawing	Religious Studies
Motor Vehicle Engineering(2,4)	Office Practice(2,4)
Commerce	Typing(3,4)
Music(1)	

Notes

1 Subject available to O-level only.
2 Subject available to CSE only.
3 Subject available to CSE and RSA only.
4 These courses are based at the East Herts College of FE.
5 An additional German group may be held in after-school time to allow sufficiently capable pupils to take extra science and two foreign languages if desired.

2 Timetable

Opposite is an extract from the 1976/7 timetable for fourth-year pupils. Subject symbols are as in structure diagram, with G, games. Note that the additional teacher in Wed. 1 & Thurs. 4, M, is extra to the team, specialising in help for slow learners.

	Wednesday 1	2	3	4	Thursday 1	2	3	4
Faculty	S	M	G	Hu	Opt B	Opt C	EA	M
	NB	BL	AS	KD	MA	JY	SH	BL
	CK	RA	JS	HL	GS	WD	JM	RA
	JFR	KN	JR	NR	WD	AP	MC	KN
X	WSS	MB	DW		JA			MB
								DP
			↓	↓	↓	↓		
Faculty	M	EA	G	Hu	Opt B	Opt C	S	EA
			↑	↑	↑	↑		
	GJS	SH	RA	JY	SC	JFR	JC	SH
	KN	DD	ES	SH	CM	KA	MW	DD
Y	AD	MC	GW	TL	WSS	MW	NB	MC
	MB						CK	
	DP							

In the above extract, X and Y denote the two half-year groups. Arrows indicate when the whole year is taught together, as a 5/6 form entry. The pattern of faculty blocking is evident.

The extract below is from the sixth-form timetable. It shows the blocked Central Studies team, and the pattern of examination subjects arranged so as to meet the combinations selected by students in consultation with careers and tutorial staff.

The full list of subjects offered is:

Advanced level Art (A), Biology (B), Chemistry (C), English (E; two parallel sets in VIi), Economics (Ec), French (F), Geography (G; two sets), German (Gmn), History (H), Home Economics (HE), Mathematics (M), Metalwork, Physics (P), Sociology (Soc) and Woodwork (total 16).

Ordinary level/CEE English, Environmental Studies, French, Geography, History, Mathematics, Metalwork, Sociology, Human Biology (HB) and Statistics (Stat) (total 10).

	Wednesday				Thursday			
	1	2	3	4	1	2	3	4
		G1					G2	
VIi A-level	E2	B	CENTRAL STUDIES			CAREERS	G1	B
		F			H			
	A	A		GAMES ETC.	HE			E1
	C				C			M
VIi O-level &CEE	A	A						
							HB	
	H	E			Stat			M
VIii A-level	A	A			HE			Soc
	F	Soc						Gmn
						G	B	G
					Ec		H	
		M					M	P

Note For clarity, the initials of staff have been omitted. At this time the total on roll was 876, including 31 in VIii and 49 in VIi. There were 54 full-time staff (including head) and 2.2 part-time.

Bibliography

Adams, A. (1976), *The Humanities Jungle*, Ward Lock Educational.
Armstrong, M. and Young, M. (1966), *The Flexible School*, Advisory Centre for Education.

Bantock, G. (1971), 'Towards a theory of popular education', in R. Hooper (ed.), *The Curriculum: Context, Design and Development*, Oliver & Boyd.
Barrow, R. (1976), *Common Sense and the Curriculum*, Unwin Education.
Becher, R. (1971), 'The dissemination and implementation of educational innovation' (unpublished), quoted in B. MacDonald and R. Walker (1976).
Benn, C. (1971), 'Making the most of RSLA', *Secondary Education*, NUT publication.
Benn, C. and Simon, B. (1972), *Half Way There*, Penguin Books.
Bennett, N. (1976), *Teaching Styles and Pupil Progress*, Open Books.
Bennis, W., Benne, K. and Chin, R. (eds) (1969), *The Planning of Change*, Holt, Rinehart & Winston.
Bernbaum, G. (1975), 'Heads see their role in tradition's mirror image', *Education*, 20 June.
Bloom, B.S. (ed.) (1956), *The Taxonomy of Educational Objectives*, Handbook I, Longmans.
Bloom, B.S. (1971), 'Mastery learning and its implications for curriculum development', in E. Eisner (ed.) (1971).
Bolton, J. and Richardson, G. (1976), 'Objective setting in education', *Education*, 4 and 11 June.
Broudy, H., Smith, B. and Burnett, J. (1965), *Democracy and Excellence in American Secondary Education*, Rand McNally.
Burstall, Clare *et al.* (1974), *Primary French in the Balance*, NFER.
Burt, Sir C. (1943), 'The education of the young adolescent: the psycho-

logical implications of the Norwood Report', *British Journal of Educational Psychology*, November.

Daunt, P. (1975), *Comprehensive Values*, Heinemann.
Davies, T. (1969), *School Organisation*, Pergamon.
De Bono, E. (1976), *Teaching Thinking*, Temple Smith.

Eisner, E. (1969), 'Instructional and expressive educational objectives: their formulation and use in curriculum', in Golby *et al.* (eds) (1975).
Eisner, E. (ed.) (1971), *Confronting Curriculum Reform*, Little, Brown.

General Studies Association (1976), *The Curriculum of the Open Sixth*, GSA Research Report.
Gilbert, J. and Egginton, L. (1976), 'A model for the evolution of a general studies programme', *General Education*, Autumn.
Golby, M., Greenwald, J. and West, R. (eds) (1975), *Curriculum Design*, Croom Helm.
Group for Research and Innovation in Higher Education (1975), *The Drift of Change*, interim report, Nuffield Foundation, also *The Times Higher Education Supplement*, 7 February.

Hamilton, D. (1976), *Curriculum Evaluation*, Open Books.
Hammersley, J. (1968), 'On the enfeeblement of mathematical skills by "Modern Mathematics" and by similar soft intellectual trash in schools and universities', *Bulletin*, Institute for Mathematics and its Applications, October.
Harris, A., Lawn, M. and Prescott, W. (eds) (1975), *Curriculum Innovation*, Croom Helm.
Harrison, M. (1976), 'Corporate management and local authority education', *Forum*, Autumn.
Hawkins, E. (1976), 'Foreign language teaching', *Trends in Education*, May.
Hirst, P. (1965), 'Liberal education and the nature of knowledge', in *Knowledge and the Curriculum* (1974), Routledge & Kegan Paul.
Hirst, P. (1967), 'The curriculum', *Schools Council Working Paper No. 12*, HMSO.
Hirst, P. (1969), 'The logic of the curriculum', *Journal of Curriculum Studies*, vol. 1, no. 2.
Hirst, P. and Peters, R. (1970), *The Logic of Education*, Routledge & Kegan Paul.
Holley, B. (1975), 'Education 16–19', *Report on Conference on Curriculum in Secondary Schools* (mimeo.), Advisory Centre for Education.
Holt, M. (1974), 'Art, craft and rational curriculum planning', *Cambridge Journal of Education*, Lent.

Holt, M. (1976), 'Non-streaming and the common curriculum', *Forum*, Spring.

Hornsby-Smith, M. (1975), 'Teaching styles in science departments', *Durham Research Review*, November.

Howson, G. (1976), 'Shape and number', *Education*, 15 October.

Hoyle, E. (1970), 'Planned organizational change in education', in A. Harris *et al.* (eds) (1975).

Hoyle, E. (1975), 'The creativity of the school in Britain', in A. Harris *et al.* (eds) (1975).

Jenkins, E. (1976), 'A new role for chemistry', *Times Educational Supplement*, 30 April.

Judge, H. (1976), 'To each according to his needs: Charles Gittins lecture', *Times Educational Supplement*, 23 April.

Kay, B. (1975), 'Monitoring pupils' performance', *Trends in Education*, July.

Kitwood, R. (1976), 'Patterns of educational research', *Studies in Higher Education*, vol. 1, no. 1.

Kogan, M. (1976), 'Democratically does it', *Times Educational Supplement*, 19 November.

Lacey, C. (1970), *Hightown Grammar*, Manchester University Press.

Lawton, D. (1973), *Social Change, Educational Theory and Curriculum Planning*, University of London Press.

Lawton, D. (1975), *Class, Culture and the Curriculum*, Routledge & Kegan Paul.

MacDonald, B. and Walker, R. (1976), *Changing the Curriculum*, Open Books.

Malpas, A. (1974), 'Objectives and cognitive demands of the SMP main school course', *Mathematics in School*, November.

Marsden, D. (1970), 'The future of comprehensive education', in D. Rubinstein and C. Stoneman (eds), *Education for Democracy*, Penguin.

Matthews, G. (1972), 'Social relevance in mathematics', *Times Educational Supplement*, 3 November.

Musgrove, F. (1971), *Patterns of Power and Authority in English Secondary Education*, Methuen.

Nuttgens, P. (1975), 'Dead hand of learning should be turned to useful skills', *Times Higher Educational Supplement*, 21 November.

Oakeshott, M. (1972), 'Education: the engagement and its frustration', in R.F. Dearden, P.H. Hirst and R.S. Peters (eds), *Education and the Development of Reason*, Routledge & Kegan Paul.

Pedley, R. *et al.* (1955), *Comprehensive Schools Today*, Councils and Education Press.

Peters, R. (1973), 'Aims of education – a conceptual inquiry', in R. Peters (ed.), *The Philosophy of Education*, Oxford University Press.

Peterson, A. (1973), *The Future of the Sixth Form*, Routledge & Kegan Paul.

Phenix, P. (1964), *Realms of Meaning*, McGraw Hill.

Pring, R. (1975), 'Integration: official policy or official fashion?', in R. Bell and W. Prescott (eds), *The Schools Council: A Second Look*, Ward Lock Education.

Punch, M. (1977), *Progressive Retreat*, Cambridge University Press.

Randall, E. (1976), 'An investigation into general studies 16–19', *General Education*, Autumn.

Reid, M. *et al.* (1974), *A Matter of Choice*, NFER.

Reid, W. and Walker, D. (eds) (1975), *Case Studies in Curriculum Change*, Routledge & Kegan Paul.

Rodgers, R. (1976), *Musical Stages*, W.H. Allen.

Rosenthal, R. and Jacobsen, L. (1968), *Pygmalion in the Classroom: Teacher Expectation and Pupils' Intellectual Development*, Holt, Rinehart & Winston.

Ross, J.M. *et al.* (1972), *A Critical Appraisal of Comprehensive Education*, NFER.

Rubinstein, D. and Simon, B. (1969), *The Evolution of the Comprehensive School*, Routledge & Kegan Paul.

School Mathematics Project (1974), *Manipulative Skills in School Mathematics*, SMP Office, Westfield College, London.

Schools Council (1970), *Sixth-form Pupils and Teachers*, NFER.

Schools Council Research Study (1973), *The Examination Courses of First Year Sixth Formers*, Macmillan.

Schwab, J. (1964), 'Structure of the disciplines: meanings and significances', in Golby *et al.* (eds) (1975).

Schwab, J. (1969), 'The practical: a language for curriculum', *School Review*, November.

Shipman, M. (1974), *Inside a Curriculum Project*, Ward Lock Educational.

Simon, B. (1974), *The Politics of Educational Reform, 1920–1940*, Lawrence & Wishart.

Skilbeck, M. (1972), 'Forms of curriculum integration', *General Education*, Spring.

Skilbeck, M. (1973), 'The school and cultural development', in Golby *et al.* (eds) (1975).

Skilbeck, M. (1976), 'School-based curriculum development', in J. Walton (ed.), *Rational Curriculum Planning*, Ward Lock Educational.

Sockett, H. (1976), *Designing the Curriculum*, Open Books.
Stenhouse, L. (1975), *An Introduction to Curriculum Development*, Heinemann.

Tawney, R. (1943), 'The problem of the public schools', in R. Hinden (ed.), *The Radical Tradition* (1966), Penguin Books.
Taylor, P.H. (1970), *How Teachers Plan Their Courses*, NFER.
Taylor, P.H., Reid, W. and Holley, B. (1974), *The English Sixth Form*, Routledge & Kegan Paul.
Taylor, W. (1973), *Heading for Change*, Routledge & Kegan Paul.

UNESCO, (1972), *Learning to Be*, Harrap.

Vernon, P. (ed.) (1957), *Secondary School Selection*, Methuen.
Voege, H. (1975), 'The diffusion of Keynesian macronomics through American high-school textbooks 1936–1970', in W. Reid and D. Walker (eds) (1975).

Warnock, M. (1973), 'Towards a definition of quality in education', in R. Peters (ed.), *The Philosophy of Education*.
Webb, Sidney (1908), 'Secondary education', in H. Binns (ed.), *A Century of Education 1808–1908*, Dent.
White, J. (1969), 'The curriculum mongers: education in reverse', in R. Hooper (ed.), *The Curriculum* (1971), Oliver & Boyd.
White, J. (1973), *Towards a Compulsory Curriculum*, Routledge & Kegan Paul.
Whitfield, R. (1971), *Disciplines of the Curriculum*, McGraw Hill.
Whitfield, R. (1973), 'Curriculum Planning', *Trends in Education*, April.
Williamson, D. (1976), 'Organisation and achievement within the comprehensive school', unpub. M. Phil. thesis, University of Surrey.
Wilson, J. (1975), *Educational Theory and the Preparation of Teachers*, NFER.
Wilson, P. (1971), *Interest and Discipline in Education*, Routledge & Kegan Paul.

Index